The World Is Waiting

The World Is Waiting

Keith Hershey

Granada Hills, CA 91344

First Printing, November, 1986

Library of Congress Catalog Card Number 86-82817
ISBN 0-940487-00-4
Copyright 1986 by Keith Hershey
Printed in the United States of America

THE WORLD IS WAITING

Don't you know the world is waiting?
  Waiting for someone like you,
  To reach out and touch them
And show them God's Word is true.

Don't you know the world is waiting?
  Waiting for someone like you,
  To reach out and love them
And tell them Jesus loves them too.

—Keith Alan Hershey

Dedicated to . . .
"The untold masses of people,
scattered throughout the nations of the world,
who are still waiting . . ."

CONTENTS

Introduction   11

One   International Awakening   13

Two   The Gospel Has No Barriers   23

Three   And the Walls Came Tumbling Down   33

Four   The Macedonian Call   45

Five   The Middle East Maze   55

Six   A Famine in the Land   69

Seven   South Africa   83

Eight   Compassion: God's Key to Evangelism   95

Nine   He That Goeth Forth Weeping . . .   107

Ten   Perfected Fruit   115

Eleven   Dear Lord, Don't Let Us Fail   125

Twelve   In the Midst of a Miracle   135

Thirteen   The Prophet's Warning . . .
                and Reward   143

Epilogue   151

INTRODUCTION

Jesus' answer to a question from His disciples has always intrigued me. Jesus said, "My meat is to do the will of him that sent me, and to finish his work. Say not ye, There are yet four months, and then cometh harvest? behold, I say unto you, Lift up your eyes, and look on the fields; for they are white already to harvest" (John 4:34,35).

Long before I entered the ministry, I was struck by Jesus' answer. And since responding to His call upon my life, these words of Jesus have powerfully motivated me to "Go ye." This book is not a biography in the truest sense of the word, but is an effort to provide the body of Christ with a greater perspective of the worldwide work of God.

The Spirit of God *is* moving mightily throughout the world's harvest field. And as each of us become sensitive to His leading we can become God's instruments to convey His wondrous redeeming love and to fulfill the Great Commission.

As you read this book I trust that God will give you "His optics" so that you may clearly see the deep needs of His people all over the world. I will be praying that the excitement of His love will capture you as you begin to realize that *God has a plan for His people, and you have a part in His plan!*

So, let's join our faith together, play the part He intends for us, and reach the entire world with His love!

—Keith Hershey, Granada Hills, California,
August 1986

1

INTERNATIONAL AWAKENING

I remember . . .

I remember preaching in Ghana . . . Malawi . . . Kenya . . . Zimbabwe . . . South Africa . . . Liberia . . . Uganda . . . and being deeply stirred as hundreds of people responded to the call of Jesus Christ. I'll never forget the urgency they expressed as they literally ran to the place of prayer to make Jesus Christ the Lord of their lives.

I remember sharing God's Word in schools and universities and being awed by the power of God as teachers and professors and staff members responded to the urging of the Holy Spirit by committing their lives to Him.

I remember watching the faces of Muslims . . . Hindus . . . Buddhists . . . as they struggled to believe the reality of Jesus' resurrection.

I remember them all: the blacks, the whites, the coloreds of Africa, bound by superstition, bound by tradition, bound by demon worship. I remember watching them cast off their yokes as the Spirit of the Living God set them free.

I remember it all. How could I ever forget the light that suddenly burst forth from within them as Jesus Christ released them from the prison houses of sin, suffering and despair. I remember them all—as they wrenched themselves free from the spell of the ancestral drums, fell into step with Jesus' Triumphal Procession and began marching to the sound of a different Drummer . . .

I remember . . .

After completing the crusades in East Africa and Liberia, Heidi returned home. Then I went into Ghana. I hadn't wanted Heidi to go home, but I knew she must. We had just completed a two-week evangelistic crusade in Liberia and East Africa which were coordinated by African evangelists. Hundreds had come to the Lord. We had both been involved every day and again every evening. And we were bone weary. Exhausted.

My decision was further prompted by the U. S. State Department reports of Ghana's political situation: uncertain. Fragile. This would be no place for my wife. A Ghanan brother, Isaac Ababio, had planned to escort me into his country. But at the last minute he found himself unable to change his flight schedule.

We looked at each other. "I'm very sorry, Keith," Isaac said, "but there is nothing I can do."

"We can telephone Jonathan," I responded, "and he can meet me at the airport."

He shook his head. "We cannot make telephone calls into Ghana . . ."

I knew then that I would have to go in alone. I didn't personally know a single soul besides Isaac in

Accra, Ghana. And because of scheduling change, nobody knew when I was coming. So there would be no one to meet me at the airport. I would be a stranger in a strange, possibly hostile land. My only consolation was that I was certain that God was directing me to go.

Though my mind was in something of turmoil during the flight, I was somewhat comforted as I thought of the Apostle Paul's answer to King Agrippa's challenge. "Therefore . . . I was not disobedient to the heavenly vision." It had been a vision of the need that had brought me to Ghana, a vision that most certainly had come from the Lord. I leaned back in my seat and closed my eyes.

Minutes later as we disembarked at Ghana's International Airport at Accra, I was struck again by a blast of the heat and humidity. My many months in Africa had made me somewhat accustomed to that. But there was something more here, something I had not experienced in all of Africa, at least to this degree. It wasn't the extreme poverty, though that was certainly evident. I had seen much poverty before. And it wasn't the armed guards. They were commonplace it Africa. It was something else.

Then it hit me. It was confusion. Oppression. It was fear. It was all around me. On the faces of the passengers. It was evidenced by the airport officials themselves. It pervaded the very atmosphere.

As always I stood tensely by while the Customs' people tore through my luggage piece by piece. Finally they were through and I stuffed my belongings back into my bags as well as I could. When I had done so and again moved through the sweaty mass of humanity, a second man accosted me. "Open your bags," he ordered.

"But they've already been passed," I protested.

"Open them!" he glared authoritatively. So I opened them and fumed inwardly as he poked and rummaged through the already disorderly contents. Finally he grunted something I couldn't understand and said. "Okay. You can go now . . ." Then he turned away as I tried to make order out of the havoc he'd created.

All the while I was sharply aware of the noise and clamor, the total confusion that pervaded the airport complex. For the second time I grabbed my bags and started for the exit. As I did I was stopped by a third man. "Step into my booth," he ordered, "Open the bags." So I wearily opened my travel-worn bags for the third time. He glanced disinterestedly at the rumpled contents and gestured for me to close them. Then he asked, "How much money do you have?"

Puzzled, I responded, "I've got $195.00."

"Let me see it."

By now I was more than a little agitated, but tried to conceal my irritation. I opened my wallet. As he reached for it he said, "How much of that are you going to give to me?"

This was more than I was prepared to handle. I felt like giving it all to him but I was prompted within to respond differently. So I said, "I'm not going to give you any of it."

He glared at me, attempting to intimidate me. This time when he spoke, his voice was petulant, whining. "But I need it to buy beer and women . . ."

By now I was righteously angry. "I'm not in your country to bribe people," I said firmly. "I've come here to share the love of the Lord Jesus Christ."

It was as though the money got hot in his hands and he handed all the monies back to me immediately. The whine left his voice and he asked where my meetings were going to be. Squaring his shoulders he quickly ushered me from his booth. This time I looked neither right nor left, but shoved my way through the beggars, the hopeful baggage carriers and taxi drivers, and out into the bright sunlight.

Not a single familiar sight or person met my eyes. "Father, what am I to do now?" I prayed.

For quite a while I stood there, being jostled and shoved by the now thinning foot traffic. Finally I heard a gentle voice beside me ask, "Sir, do you need help?"

The black face showed friendly concern. Somehow I knew we were brothers. "Yes," I told him, "I am looking for the office of a man who lives in Accra and is a Gospel evangelist."

"Perhaps I know him . . . what's his name?"

"Isaac Ababio, of the Hour of Visitation Evangelistic Association."

The black face wreathed itself in a wonderful smile. "I know him," he said. "Here is my truck . . . I'll take you to his office."

I relaxed against the seat of my new friend's truck, while he skillfully wound his way through the dirty streets of the deteriorating capitol city of Ghana. A far cry from Amsterdam, I thought as I remembered . . .

#   #   #

Bustling, busy Amsterdam. Neat and orderly Amsterdam!

Boats and ship canals. Thousands of bicycles. Rows and rows of tiny, neatly-kept houses. Beside me, Heidi had caught her breath. "I've never seen anything like it!"

I smiled down at her. This was my first time in The Netherlands also and I, too, was loving it. Every minute of it. Streams of people were making their way into the huge auditorium: people of every color and dress. My wife and I joined ourselves with them. We were aware that a score of unfamiliar languages was flowing around us.

I understood none of it: except the universal excitement. We jostled our way with the joyous, expectant flow into the meeting room. I gasped as I caught sight of the huge banner—AMSTERDAM was in bold print. To those who understood, that banner told it all. It was the culmination of Billy Graham's dream, the bringing together of the world's itinerant evangelists, God's proclaimers of His Word. Heidi and I found a seat and sat down amongst them.

As I did, an exuberancy welled up within me. I, too, was an evangelist. I, too, had accepted Christ's command to go into all the world. I, too, had a calling to fulfill. And in the days that followed, I became a part of those others. I saw them, met them, rubbed elbows with them, wept with them, prayed with them—these men and women from "every nation, every language from under the sun . . ."

And even as Pentecost had shaken the entire world, I knew that the Amsterdam Conference would shake the world. I thought, Heidi and I are a part of all this—we're part of God's plan to take His Son, Jesus to the nations . . ."

I felt a quickening in my spirit as I read the theme of this international gathering—"Do the work of an Evangelist" (II Timothy 4:5)—the admonition the Apostle Paul gave to Timothy, his young fellow laborer in the faith. Being quite young in age myself, I identified with Timothy, and I too, received these words the Apostle Paul had given to him. Day after day during the Amsterdam Conference those words rang in my heart and I determined to accept that command to Timothy as my own.

This was my first assignment as a young missionary. My task was to journey through Europe, the Middle East and Africa for the purpose of meeting Christian leaders in addition to doing the work of the ministry in evangelistic campaigns.

The reason behind those meetings was of great importance. I was to discuss the possibility of gathering key Christian leaders—both Arabs and Jews—from the Mediterranean perimeter for a historic conference.

"It's an impossible task!" I heard again and again during my weeks of preparation before leaving the United States.

One prominent Christian leader just shook his head. "Do you actually know what you're getting yourself into? That Middle East situation is so explosive that nobody even knows to begin to approach those believers with such an idea!"

I shook my head. "No, I don't know what I'm getting into. But I am confident in this—that when the Spirit of God is directing you, and the doors of ministry in these areas are beginning to open, then . . . you cannot help but go."

I must admit I was very naive about the whole Middle East situation. And I didn't have the slightest concept of what I would be getting into. However, the very thought of fellowshiping with these key believers ignited my soul and set it ablaze with excitement! So when the opportunity had presented itself, I shared it with my lovely wife of two months. Heidi and I discussed the matter for weeks as we opened ourselves up to the Lord. In the end it seemed clear that the Lord was directing us, and we agreed to go.

Michael Cassidy, one of those igniting this ministry in the Middle East, was delighted with our decision. And when he briefed me he said, "Keith, this is a Joshua-and-Caleb assignment. It's very similar to the assignment God gave those men when He sent them to scout out the land for the Children of Israel."

He paused to note the effect of his words before he went on. I felt my heart pounding. What did Michael mean, I wondered, scout out the land? I was soon to learn.

"I want you to go where the Spirit of God leads you," he said. "And as did Joshua and Caleb, you will need to obtain a visual perspective before moving into the land. So I can't give you much guidance. But your assignment," Michael continued, "if you choose to accept it, is to gain the vital information and in-sight that's needed to put together a conference that will bring these Middle East and Mediterranean church leaders together . . ."

Michael Cassidy is no novice at this business. As a South African born evangelist, Michael founded African Enterprise over 20 years ago, with the single objective of winning Africa for Christ. Along with his Co-Team Leader, Bishop Festo Kivengere of Uganda, Michael has been used of the Lord in new and unique ways to do just that. They have dared to follow the Lord's leading and to intervene in some of Africa's most explosive political situations with the healing Gospel of reconciliation.

Knowing Michael's track record, I believed that this bold and daring venture of ours had been birthed because of his sensitivity to the leading of the Holy Spirit.

As I meditated upon the Scriptures dealing with Joshua's daring adventure into the unknown, I determined that if I was to accept an assignment such as his, that I would also expect the same kind of results: a good report, despite the giants I might encounter in the land of the Philistines.

Before embarking upon this adventure I realized that the association with thousands of the world's evangelists would provide me with invaluable information. And immeasurable insight. Where else could this be found than at the Amsterdam Conference?

Billy Graham's opening address set the pace that never slackened throughout the entire conference. Speaking on, "The Evangelist in a Broken World," Dr. Graham skillfully described the frontlines I would soon be facing.

Dr. Paul Yonggi Cho's message, "The Evangelist and the Life of Faith," reminded me that I must lift up the Lord and look to His Word for solutions and victory in all the desperate circumstances I would face on the battlefield. One by one, each of those godly warriors who shared their battle strategies with us contributed to the fresh infilling I needed before I completed my preparations to invade enemy territory.

2

THE GOSPEL HAS NO BARRIERS

Those ten days in Amsterdam inalterably changed my life! Never again could I be unaware of the vastness of our world. Nor of the billions, yes *billions*, of living, breathing, struggling human beings, scarcely any different than myself, who were marking time and *waiting* for someone to come and tell them that God loves them, and that He sent Jesus Christ to redeem them from their darkness and from their bondage! During those gripping days, statistics came alive for me. I learned that . . .

Nearly four and one-half billion *people* inhabit our globe.

Nearly two and one-half billion of those *people* have never heard an effective, viable witness of the Gospel.

Only six percent of the world's population are active Christians. And of the believers, there is only one Christian worker for every 450,000 *people* who have never heard!

There are over 7,000 living languages in the world today, and of that number, over 5,000 of them have no Bible in their own language.

I was shocked to learn that 80,000 unsaved *people* die every single day. That's 3,333 every hour, 55 every minute. All of them destined for a Christless eternity!

Realizing these facts helped put my own assignment into a better perspective. I looked around me. What a priceless group I was a part of! What a tremendous "cloud of witnesses." And all of them blending all their efforts to win the world for Jesus. I was proud to be a part of such a gathering.

How I praise God for the fellowship of His saints Heidi and I enjoyed during the conference at Amsterdam. Over 4,500 of God choice men and women: ready and willing to go, to speak, to share, to give of themselves so that others could receive the blessings of God's love which they had received.

With such a dynamic group as this, evangelistic fervor had to have an outlet. So we were organized into small groups to take our precious message to the people of Amsterdam.

The results were predictable.

After that day in the field, Heidi and I were trading experiences with an evangelist from India. He was effervescent with joy. "The Gospel has no barriers!" he said.

I agreed with an appropriate, "Amen, Brother."

"Here I am," he continued, "a dark-skinned East Indian, sharing Jesus with the light-skinned Dutch people . . . *and they listened to me*! he said in amazement. "And not only did they listen to me, but they were receptive to my message . . . and three of them opened their hearts to Jesus and were born again! Praise God!"

The experiences Heidi and I had paralleled those of our Indian friend. "It didn't matter that I was from India . . ." he said, "the Lord used me just the same."

I agreed. "And it didn't matter that we are from America," I said, "and that we don't speak Dutch. The Dutch people responded to us also."

During that one day alone, untold scores of people came to Jesus as the "fired-up" evangelists went out from their sessions and seminars to put into practice what they'd been hearing.

I thought of the week prior to the conference at Amsterdam when Heidi and I had met for several days with members of the African Enterprise team. In company with a number of African evangelists from every corner of Africa, we had convened in the small Dutch village of Burgh-Haamstede to stategize methods for winning Africa to the Lord. These men and women of God had come together to for a single purpose: evangelism.

Evangelism to their individual countries. And evangelism of the entire continent! What a vision. Many times during that week we'd spontaneously break into singing the song that has burned itself into my heart, and has almost become my theme song—"Africa Belongs to God."

On the surface the task of winning the entire continent of Africa might seem impossible. But not to these nationals. One could tell by the expressions upon their intent, glowing faces and by the seriousness of their sparse words that not for a moment did they consider the task too large.

These men and women knew their God, and in

His name were doing exploits.

Time and again as I watched and listened to them, I was reminded of the young man David preparing himself for his encounter with the "impregnable" Goliath.

David was appalled by the reaction of Israel's soldiers when they saw their nemesis. "He's too strong . . . too big!"

But David's response was different. On numerous occasions he'd been empowered by God to overcome his enemies: the lion, the bear. Time and again, by utilizing God's strength, he'd destroyed those who'd come to destroy his father's sheep. He *knew* His God. He knew Who lived within him.

Those soldiers shouted, "Goliath's too big!"

David chuckled. "Yes, he is too big. He's too big a target to miss!" For David knew His God. And he knew he would not go into the fray in his own strength alone. He would go out against Goliath *in the name of the Lord of hosts, the Lord of manifested power.* And David knew that by doing so he could not fail.

These African evangelists viewed their task in the same light that David had. And I knew that if I were to succeed, and if I were to overcome the Goliaths I would be facing, that I must do the same.

During those days at the Amsterdam Conference I was involved in numerous meetings with Middle East Christian leaders, the purpose of which was, in part, to plan a major thrust into Lebanon. Then, as now, those were perilous days in Lebanon. And we took into account the fact that bombs and guns were even then destroying lives and property throughout the land.

But even more destructive than these modern weapons of warfare were the most insidious weapons of all: the more ancient weapons of deceit, hate, revenge that had prevailed for centuries between the Jews and Arabs.

Could a war against such formidable weapons be won?

We put the subject of the Lebanon mission on the shelf and began to discuss the possibility of having church leaders from the entire Middle East gather together in fellowship.

I sat in silence as these Mid-East leaders hunched earnestly over tables. "It's dangerous," they agreed. "To attempt to bring together Christian Arabs and Christian Jews in any country would only pour more gasoline upon the fire?"

Why? I wondered. They answered my unspoken question.

"It would bring more bloodshed," they agreed amongst themselves. "It would anger the Muslim governmental leaders and heap even more persecution upon the heads of the Arab Christian community . . ."

John Wilson, an African evangelist residing in Kenya, though a Ugandan by birth, spoke. His calm voice was like a healing balm in the tense planning session. "Our purpose is not to evangelize the Muslims," he said, "nor to meddle in politics . . ."

"Then what is our purpose?" one brother challenged.

John smiled. "We're to be God's vessels . . . His vessels of love . . . to assist the body of Christ in this region. All we want to do is to help them get their eyes off the fighting, the bloodshed, and to envision the work of the resurrected Lord. And then they'll be able to see each other as brothers. Then healing can

27

take place . . ."

He paused to allow this to sink in. Then his low-pitched voice came to us again. "Perhaps we could call this mission, 'From Africa with Love.' "

By now John had their attention. As he leaned toward them to share the plan in greater detail, they responded to him with respect. "I know that the situation is explosive," he said, "but I am convinced that the timing is right . . . God's timing."

I saw heads nodding in agreement. I, too, was listening intently, because I needed to learn how to accomplish a task that even these seasoned Mid-Eastern leaders thought impossible.

"We must not discuss prophetic interpretations of Scripture concerning Israel and her Scriptural destiny," John said. "We must not get caught in such a trap . . ."

John Wilson paused and looked around the circle, catching each man's eye one at a time. "If this task is to succeed we must minister only God's love, from His corporate household . . . and we must do so without theological barriers. Because we will be dealing with those of the most Fundamental and evangelical, with the liberals and Pentecostals, and with the old, main-line Orthodox. Our task is to work with them all . . . to pull them all together. To bind them into one cohesive Body of Christ . . ."

I learned much from John.

Sitting there, watching and listening, knowing that it was John who was spearheading this action, I was amazed at his warm diplomacy and skill. The way he was enabled to avoid and ease sensitive issues in what was and is to the world a very complex, muddy situation.

Not once did John Wilson express anything but love toward his Arab brothers. And they responded to that love, as all men eventually respond to love. It was because of that love that they heard his words and respected his wisdom. And in the end, it was largely because of their love and trust for John that we decided to accept the challenge of unifying the Christian leaders of the Middle East . . .

As the Amsterdam Conference began winding down and the final seminars and sessions approached, I suddenly realized that I had been in training for conflict. But soon I would be going into battle. The "briefings" that John Wilson and the others had given me had been to equip me for the day when Heidi and I would be on our own. And that like Joshua and Caleb, we'd be pushing toward a new, as yet untested frontier.

I began enumerating the obstacles. There were many to overcome. I viewed the mountain ranges between me an my goal. They were high and plentiful and must be removed or tunnelled through.

Because God's Golden Open Door lay before me.

"No man shall be able to stand before you . . ." God told Joshua. "As I was with Moses, so I will be with you. I will not leave you nor forsake you."

Since I was embarking upon a Joshua-Caleb-type assignment, I took God's promise to Joshua as my own.

When a young-man-size project became available in Hebron, the now elderly Caleb claimed it. He said to Joshua, "I am as strong this day as I was on the day that Moses sent me . . ."

Joshua knew what his fellow warrior was talking about. He had been there that day when Moses had sent them both out to spy out the land of the giants. He nodded, having an inkling of what his friend was going to say.

"Just as my strength was then," Caleb went on, "so *now is my strength for war*. . . . Now, therefore give me this mountain of which the Lord spoke . . ."

Joshua must have believed mightily in Caleb, for he honored his friend's request: he gave him the mountain to conquer.

I thought about Joshua and Caleb. I thought about the humanly impossible challenges they had accepted. And how—with the total resources of their mighty God behind them—they had fulfilled their missions with honor.

I thought of Michael Cassidy's charge to me. Even as Moses had entrusted those critically-important assignments to Joshua and Caleb, Michael had entrusted this one to me. Could I do it? Yes, I could do it, because I had at my disposal the same resources that had been available to them.

From the depth of my heart, from the totality of my being, I spoke to God, "Father, send me into the territory . . . give me that mountain."

And when I made that commitment to God that day, it included more than just the Middle East assignment. It included that, but it included more. I had in mind all of the endless opportunities for outreach and evangelism and ministry that I was confident my Father would lay before me as I was faithful.

Again I very soberly vowed, "Father, give me that mountain—*that mountain* and *those other mountains*—for in Your strength, in Your power I am able!"

Almost abruptly, the Amsterdam Conference was over, and Heidi and I were actually on our way. I must admit to a tingle of excitement as we launched out into the unknown. We boarded the plane to cross the Channel into England to begin our first phase of this assignment, on the way to Africa.

The words of David Livingstone filled my mind: ". . . no reservation, no regret, and no retreat."

3

AND THE WALLS CAME TUMBLING DOWN

When we arrived in London, I began contacting key Christian leaders to seek the benefit of their wise counsel concerning ministry in the Middle East. I found these busy men most congenial and generous with their time. One of the most helpful was Dr. Tom Houston, then president of the London Bible Society, and now president of World Vision International.

Though physically small of stature, I found Dr. Houston to be a giant in his understanding of the world scene. When I met him in the bustling office of the London Bible Society, he quickly put me at ease. He offered me lunch, which I accepted, and when we had been served, he said, "And now, Keith, how can I be of service to you?"

I explained to him my Middle East assignment, ending with, "Basically, I believe we are to be a bridge between nations and cultures . . . and to communicate the Gospel of reconciliation."

Dr. Houston took another bite of his salad before he answered. Then in his unique, soft-spoken manner, he gently probed for more information. "With the various political and religious views that abound in the Mediterranean region, you must clarify for yourself which of these bridges you want to cross . . ."

He peered at me through his very British-looking glasses. "So tell me this, Keith, which area of communication do you wish to emphasize?"

"Basically unity of the body of Christ," I said.

He nodded. "In addition there are other areas you might wish to consider," he said, "such as mutual love for the citizens of other nations. Or simply the recognition of the basic rights and privileges of those other peoples. And again you might get them to dialogue their concept of Biblical authority in each of their own cultures . . . to name a few."

My two hours with Dr. Houston were soon ended. And as I thanked him and took my leave, I realized that his sound advice would certainly stand me in good stead.

A mutual acquaintance had suggested I telephone Victor Hashweh, an Arab believer now living in London. After I introduced myself and advised him of the purpose of my call, he, too, responded warmly.

"This is indeed providential," he said. "Because next week we're having a week-long Arab Christian Conference outside of London. There'll be Arab believers from Jordan, Egypt, Lebanon and various European countries attending. Why don't you and your wife join us?"

The doors were opening sooner that I had dared hope for! "That sounds great!" I responded enthusiastically. "Just tell me when and where and we'll be there."

"The conference is being held at Ashburnham Place, an old English estate," Victor told me, "and if you'd like, you can ride out there on our bus with us." I quickly accepted his offer. So it was, a few days later, that Heidi and I found ourselves enjoying a ride into the English hinterlands with a busload of Christian Arabs.

We quickly realized that we were the only Western couple on the bus, and thus very definitely in the minority. With everyone else speaking rapidly in Arabic, pausing now and then to glance quizzically in our direction, we had the uncomfortable feeling that they were wondering what we doing here with them.

It wasn't long before our suspicions were confirmed. An elderly, quite distinguished-looking lady in her 70's, moved close to Heidi and struck up a conversation with her.

"Do you know the Lord?" the lady asked.

"Yes," my wife responded, "I've had a relationship with Jesus as my Lord for several years now."

The old woman fixed Heidi with a stern look. "You need to know that we've all sinned and need to be saved . . ." With these words, the woman introduced her lengthy monologue concerning Heidi's salvation. Heidi listened patiently, occasionally trying to speak of few words to reaffirm her commitment to the Lord. Now and then she'd turn to me with a puzzled look on her face.

I, too, was puzzled. Then, quite suddenly, it dawned on me: we had quite innocently violated some strict Arab cultural taboos. Heidi was wearing makeup, which was forbidden. Because the day was quite warm, she was wearing a sleeveless sundress: another taboo. An Arab woman's shoulders must never be exposed in public. Better still, her arms should be completely covered.

Heidi looked at me helplessly. There was nothing I could do.

It was then that a young woman came to Heidi's rescue. She was seated close to Heidi and introduced herself. "My name is Jinetta," she said.

Heidi gratefully turned toward Jinetta. "My name's Heidi. And this is my husband, Keith."

"This seems to be your first experience in an Arab culture," Jinetta observed with a warm smile. She told us she was from the West Indies, but had moved to London where she met and married an Egyptian engineering student. The two young women enjoyed each other's fellowship for much of the rest of our journey.

The time passed quickly and we soon found ourselves turning onto a long, tree-lined gravel driveway that led to the spectacular conference center. The main building of the center consisted of a huge, well-kept traditional British estate, surrounded by several acres of manicured gardens that were a joy to behold and appeared to be a restful strolling place.

After disembarking from the bus, Heidi and I mingled with the others and introduced ourselves. As we did, one of the Arab brothers addressed us abruptly, "I see that your wife likes that blue soap."

"Blue soap?" I said. "What do you mean?"

"*Blue soap*," he said, indicating Heidi's makeup. "She'd look a lot better without it . . ."

I was irritated by the man's abrasive words and manner, but under the circumstances, there was nothing I could do. Apparently completely unaware, or uncaring of either Heidi's or my feelings, he had even more to say.

"In fact, I'm not sure if God will allow people wearing that blue soap into heaven."

I gently smiled and as tactfully as possible I changed the subject, and as soon as we could gracefully do so, Heidi and I fled to our room. She was hurt and angry. I was upset and discouraged. How could I ever hope to reach these people about whose customs I knew so little? It took me a long time to get to sleep that night.

From that beginning, as far as I was concerned, the conference got off to a bad start. It seemed to be "us and them," instead of "we," as I had hoped it would be. I knew that it was crucial for me to dialogue with these Arab people if I was to obtain any of the information I desperately needed. Yet with each contact the walls separating us seemed to grow higher and the distance between us greater.

We did everything we could think of to build a bridge between us. Heidi toned down her makeup and changed her wardrobe—all apparently to no avail.

It seemed that we had been categorized and labelled. Since we were Western in origination, we were automatically pigeonholed both politically and theologically. They naturally assumed us to be pro-Israel in every sense of the word, which meant that we had little if any real regard or concern for the Arab world in general, or the Palestinian problem in particular.

What could I do? I searched my soul and agonized in prayer. But for days the outcome was zero.

After one of the older Arab leaders from the Middle East had ministered, I approached him. "Sir," I began, "could I spend a few moments with you to gain some insight into the Church's problems in the Middle East?"

He listened coldly. Without looking me in the eye, he gave me an inconsequential answer and walked away.

By the third day of the conference we seemed to have reached an impasse and I was truly concerned.

That morning I could stand the stress no longer. I slipped out of one of the sessions to walk in the garden and commune with the Lord. Oblivious to anything about me, I was startled when I heard someone call my name. I turned. It was Victor, the man who had organized the conference and who had invited us to come.

"Oh, good morning, Victor," I said.

Quite pleasantly, he asked, "How has your time been?"

"Most interesting," I answered cautiously, wondering if Victor was aware of the wall between me and the others.

"The Lord is certainly moving in the Muslim world," he said, and began telling me of a number of amazing events that had been transpiring among Arab believers in the Middle East. "As a result," he concluded, "many Muslims are coming to the Lord."

Of course I was very pleased to hear these reports, but in the back of my mind was the question, "With my inability to communicate with these Arabs in England, how can I possibly have a part with those in the Middle East?"

Suddenly I was aware that Victor was looking at me quite intently. "Keith," he began, "do you have a message on your heart that you'd like to share with this conference?"

Briefly taken aback by the abruptness of the question, I stammered a reply. "Well . . . well, yes. Yes. Certainly. In fact, Victor, the Lord *has* been dealing with me about a certain matter that I would like to share with these people."

Victor smiled broadly. "Good. One of our speakers—the one who was to speak tomorrow morning—informed us that he can't be here. Could you speak in his place tomorrow morning?"

"I'd be happy to do so, Victor. Very happy. And . . . thanks for the invitation."

With a smile and "God bless you," Victor was gone, leaving me praising the Lord for this new opportunity. Whereas, just minutes before I had been agonizing in seeming defeat, now I was rejoicing in hope.

The next morning after being introduced, speaking through an interpreter, I shared with my listeners the process and results of the spiritual inventory I had recently taken. "I asked the Lord why my life and personal ministry were not more vibrant manifestations of His love . . . of His glory," I told them.

"I asked God why I wasn't experiencing the abundance of the life that Jesus had declared was already mine . . ."

I told them of my personal struggles, of agonizing over the seeming failure of my walk with the Lord. "It often seemed to me that bitterness . . . resentment . . . unforgiveness . . . and other manifestations of the old man, the old nature . . . were sometimes taking the upper hand in my walk with the Lord . . ."

As I spoke, I recognized the presence of the Spirit of God. Hardly a man or woman moved. As one person they leaned toward me in an effort not to miss a single word. In a flash of revelation I realized that I was touching on a universal truth. These Arab brothers and sisters were identifying with me. My spiritual problems and agonies were the same as theirs. They were hearing the words that came from my mouth, but they were listening to the voice of the Lord.

Suddenly another fact became evident to me: even as they were opening their hearts to receive from the Lord—the partition, the high walls that had separated us throughout this conference, were crumbling before my very eyes!

I likened my situation to that of Lazarus. When Jesus had spoken to the decaying brother of Mary and Martha from the mouth of the tomb, He commanded, "Lazarus, come forth!"

That had been the beginning of the miracle.

"Then he that was dead came forth, bound hand and foot with grave clothes . . ." (John 11:44).

I paused there, remembering the depth of my own struggle. "It was at this particular place that the Lord spoke to me," I said. "He told me, 'Keith, many of My people have been resurrected, but are not yet released! Many people, though they have been born again, are still bound!' "

I enumerated the bonds the Spirit of God had shown me that still immobilized me, and many others of His own people. There were the bonds of habits . . . of jealousy . . . of strife . . . of fear . . . the spirit of inferiority. And also the spirit of superiority.

"Dead men's clothing comes in many forms," I continued. "Some people have hatred and resentment against those of other colors, other cultures, other nations or races. And this hatred and resentment in the hearts of God's people means they are still bound in dead men's clothing!"

As I poured out my heart to my Arab brothers and sisters, there was a confidence within me that it was not I, but God Who was speaking.

"My friends, don't remain bound in dead men's clothing," I urged. "Because, if you do, Jesus Christ will remain imprisoned within you. His love and power will be unable to be expressed through your lives. And like I found myself, you will be miserable and empty, wondering about your own Christian faith . . ."

As the Lord had revealed them to me, I shared with my new friends the principles for walking in the realm of release and joining the Triumphal Procession with Jesus.

When I finally sensed it was time to close, I invited those who desired to be freed from their dead men's clothes and bondage to raise their hands. I was stunned to note that more than three-quarters of the listeners responded.

What followed was one of those rare times when God's people open their hearts in concert before Him: weeping, repenting, then rejoicing as they sense the release of the Holy Spirit . . .

I knew as I arose from my knees that the walls that had stood between us had come tumbling down, and that the barriers were gone. And almost before the session was behind us, Heidi and I found ourselves besieged by those who had previously ignored us. "Tell us more . . . we must know more . . . will you pray for me" was the almost universal cry of those who approached us.

It was such a reversal in attitude that we hardly

knew how to respond. And we praised God for the new openness we were now experiencing with these Arab brothers.

Following that morning session, I will never forget the long, leisurely walks I took through the wooded hillsides with those Arab Christian leaders whom, mere hours or days before, would not open up to me. But now, thank God, in the quiet, peaceful setting of the rolling English countryside, and the lush beauty of the estate's formal gardens, we conferred about how best to present the Prince of Peace to the strife-torn Middle East.

And as these men, many of whom had physically suffered for their faith, opened up to me I learned more of the history of the Middle East that I had ever read in textbooks. Wrung from their hearts, I felt as well as heard their concern for their own nations, and for Israel, which they still called Palestine. From these dark-skinned, men of God, I began to understand the immensity of the problems they faced . . .

And the immensity of the problems I would face—far deeper and complex than I had ever imagined—as I ventured into what was for me "the land of the giants."

It was during the closing days of the conference that Alfred asked me to help him share Jesus with his Muslim friend. From Sudan, Alfred was a young, dynamic evangelist who had somehow persuaded his friend to join him here at Ashburnham Place. Abdula, a staunch Muslim, was very knowledgeable of the Koran as well as the Bible, including the teaching of Jesus. The two of us spent hours with Abdula discussing the relevancy of Jesus Christ.

One of the last mornings of the conference Alfred

came to me, weeping profusely. I had never seen my friend in such a state and was alarmed. "What is it, Alfred?" I asked. "What's wrong?"

"Abdula," Alfred managed to say between sobs. "Abdula . . ."

"Abdula? What's happened to him?"

"He's gone . . . gone. We failed."

"Gone?" I asked. "Gone where? Where did he go?"

"I don't know where he went. He just left. During the night. Without telling me or anyone." He rocked back and forth in his grief. "My friend Abdula is gone . . . gone. And we failed him."

Not knowing what else to do, I put my arm around my Arab brother. What could I say or do, that would help relieve his grief? Alfred had prayed so hard, and so long, for his friend. We both had tried to win him to the Lord. Yet, it all seemed in vain. Why? I asked myself.

That day as I shared my friend's pain and loss, I became aware as never before of one of the most difficult hindrances of ministering in the Muslim world: their non-acceptance of the Messiahship of Jesus.

In that dark hour the words of the Apostle Paul came to me—"My little children, for whom I labor in birth . . . until Christ is formed in you" (Galatians 4:19).

Alfred's desire for his friend was that he be saved, that "Christ be formed" in Abdula. The great Apostle's desire for the world's peoples was that they be saved. In that moment of meditation I saw more clearly than I had ever seen before, that such a desire would be expensive. It would cost a great deal of something. And that something was prayer. Without prevailing prayer, a "heart's desire" for ministry would be powerless, a mere work of the flesh, self-motivated and fruitless for the Kingdom of God.

So, in order for the ministry of evangelism to produce viable fruit, it must be generated and sustained by prayer, by an overwhelming, all-consuming desire to see Christ reproduced in the lives of the Muslims . . . or the Hindus . . . or in any other cultural or ethnic or religious group.

That would be Alfred's secret of success with Abdula or any others of his Muslim friends.

That would be my own secret of success in the Middle East—or any other place in the world—the near-desperate desire that the salvation of God encompass those to whom I was ministering. And that God's salvation (*soteria* in Greek, meaning healing, preservation, deliverance and soundness of mind), the complete redemption of Jesus be formed in every area of each life: body, soul and spirit.

When this truth became apparent to me, I realized I would see my own heart's desire expand, and that then, through God's redemptive possibilities, I would be able to reach into and succeed in the most difficult situations, no matter how impossible they might appear.

During those moments that I spent with Alfred, who was still weeping like a child, it seemed that I was caught up into the very presence of God, and He was doing surgery on me. Drastic, radical heart surgery. In which he literally enlarged my heart and gave me a greater desire to see people—all kinds of people, people of all nations—experience His great salvation.

My heart, my life have never been the same. And with that new, enlarged heart that He gave me in that moment, I was able to help console the broken-hearted man I held in my arms.

4

THE MACEDONIAN
CALL

Moments after takeoff we were high over the English
Channel—on our way to Paris. Heidi snapped on her
reading light. "I think I'll look at a magazine."

Reading was the farthest thing from my mind. Our
Middle East ministry, which had begun so painfully
had taken an unexpected turn.

At the close of the conference, Victor had asked
me to meet with him and a number of the other Arab
leaders. Somewhat puzzled by the request, I was soon
to be enlightened.

Getting right to the point, Victor said, "We all
think you should go directly to France . . ."

"To France?" I echoed, not at all certain of what
he meant.

"Yes," Victor nodded vigorously, with the others in
obvious agreement, "we think you should go to
France and minister to our Arab brothers and sisters."

"In France?" I said, "but our plans are to minister
to the Arabs in the Middle East."

Victor smiled. "Brother Keith, Paris *is* the Middle East. There are more than one million Arabs living in that city alone. And they need you, they need to hear what you have been sharing with us." I couldn't mistake the deep sincerity in his face and voice. "Will you go, Keith?" he asked. "Will you go over to Paris and help them?"

A shiver of holy anticipation crept up my spine. My brothers and sisters in Paris were calling to me. Could this be my Macedonian call?"

I peered into the intense eyes of Victor and the others. Surely the request of these godly men represented the voice of God. I mentally shifted gears, something I was learning to do as I grew more and more sensitive to the leading of the Holy Spirit. I hesitated only a moment.

"Yes, Victor, I'll be glad to go to Paris."

With this Macedonian Call—"Come over into Paris and help us!"—thundering in my mind, I couldn't sleep. I couldn't even read.

The Macedonian Call!

Already, just weeks after receiving my assignment, I was actually involved in God's plan for the Middle East: the urgently needed ministry of reconciliation. I realized I was in good company: none other than the Apostle Paul. Because, along with him, and those other pioneers who had taken this all-important message into Asia, I was also a "minister of reconciliation." I was an "ambassador for Christ" (II Corinthians 5:18-20)!

It was an overwhelming concept. *Ambassador for Jesus Christ*! Entrusted with the blessed privilege of being His spokesman, a human messenger to convey His divine message. But I wasn't alone in this privilege. It was a calling, an opportunity that was available for anybody, in fact for *everybody* in the family of God, for all who are a part of His New Creation!

There on the airplane on the way to minister, I felt a tingle of excitement creep over me. I was now an ambassador-at-large for God. And I was on assignment for and under the direction of the Holy Spirit, to take His simple, yet life-changing message to the world!

I recalled Solomon's wise word that "a faithful ambassador brings healing" (Proverbs 13:17). And that was exactly what I intended to do: to help bring healing and restoration to the nations I would soon be involved with. Praise God!

I heard the captain's announcement. We were approaching our destination. "Paris, here we are," I whispered. "Ready or not, here we come . . ."

I leaned over and nudged my very engrossed wife. "Heidi . . . Heidi, we're here. We're getting ready to land in Paris." She looked up surprisedly and closed her magazine. I leaned toward the window to catch a glimpse of our Macedonia.

Our excitement at arriving in France soon turned to frustration. I telephoned Willie, our Paris contact. In his broken, yet quite understandable broken English, he urged us to come and have lunch with him. Our frustration began with our attempt to locate Willie. After a long subway ride, we found ourselves blinking uncertainly in the intense light of the midday sun.

Where were we to go from there?

Heidi and I turned first this way and that in our efforts to find Willie's home. Even the map, with everything in French, seemed of little value. Though I knew we were in the right neighborhood, I could not locate the right address.

After passing the same corner several times, I gave up in hopeless confusion. "What are you going to do?" Heidi asked me.

"I'm going to find someone who speaks English and ask for directions," I said.

About that time two young teenage boys happened by. "Pardon me," I began, "do either of you speak English?"

"I do," one of them spoke up. And, eager to practice the language, he asked, "How can I help you?"

"We're trying to locate this address," I said, handing him Willie's instructions. The two chattered in French for a moment, then the English-speaking boy said, "We'll take you there."

As we walked, our guide asked us the purpose of our visit to Paris. Apparently the other boy understood more English than he could speak, because when Heidi answered, our guide didn't have to translate for him.

Heidi told them, "We've come to tell people about Jesus."

"But, why?" they asked. "We know about Jesus."

"We want everyone to know Him personally," she said. And since they seemed to be interested, Heidi shared the way of salvation with our new-found friends.

In much less time than we had wandered after disembarking from the subway, the boys stopped in front of Willie's home. We thanked them and rewarded them with some pieces of Christian literature and a copy of the Gospel of John.

At our knock, Willie greeted us warmly. "Come in. Come in," he insisted, taking Heidi's bags from her. After giving us a brief tour of his home, Willie seated us in his pleasant, though somewhat rundown living

room. And then served us a welcome, and very refreshing cup of tea. After we had somewhat relaxed,
Willie served us a simple, but delicious luncheon.
Heidi and I found ourselves liking Willie immediately.

Born in Egypt and educated as an eye surgeon,
Willie left his medical practice to press the urgent
claims of the Gospel upon his Arab compatriots.
Though an Arab himself, during his years of living in
Paris, Willie he had acquired a number of French
mannerisms. And as with most French people we
met, Willie was gregarious and talkative, and used
his hands as well as his mouth when he talked.

Willie's special ministry, we soon learned, was primarily to assist and encourage Muslim converts. He
told us that new Arab believers are hated, rejected
and persecuted by their own people when they come
to the Lord. Their families and the Muslim community as a whole disowns them and considers them as
dead. Because of that fact, Willie's home had become
a haven, a literal "hiding place" for these harassed
new believers. I was surprised to note that as many
as 20 different people could be "housed" at one time
in the numerous cracks and crevices that Willie had
ingeniously built into his home.

As Willie talked, I was again reminded of the stories Corrie ten Boom told of hiding Jewish families
from the SS during World War II. And I remembered
how her family paid the ultimate price for their compassion. Though the time and place were different
for Willie, and those he hid and protected were Arabs
instead of Jews, in many regards the risks he took
compared with those that Corrie and her family took.

During our tour of his home, Willie had shown us
a room that contained numerous stacks of books,
and that appeared to be set up as a classroom. "This

is where we teach the new believers to walk with God," he explained. "We teach them regularly. And since some of the people must remain here for several days, we often take advantage of the time by conducting seminars."

Our host related a number of stories of his work in Paris, of many, many who had given up Islam and made Jesus of Nazareth Lord of their lives. According to Jesus' command, Willie would witness to and then teach these Muslims until they opened their hearts to Jesus. Then he would baptize the converts, and continue to teach them until they were firmly grounded in the life-giving Word of the Living God.

As we concluded our rooftop luncheon and Willie his story, I spoke up. "What a fabulous ministry you have, Willie!"

Willie acknowledged the compliment with a smile and a slight nod. He was pensively silent for a moment, then he looked up and surprised me with his next words. "Keith, will you preach in my Arab church tomorrow, Sunday afternoon?"

"Well, yes. Yes, of course. I'd be happy to do so."

"We'll be pleased to hear your message from the Lord," he said. "The service is at 4:00 o'clock," he told me, "and here's the location." He wrote the address on a piece of paper. Then, after spending a time of prayer with Willie, Heidi and I went on our way rejoicing.

The following afternoon we set out early to find Willie's church, and finally found it. The small room that had been made available to them by an evangelistic mission was located in a cul-de-sac. Heidi and I arrived early and were amazed as we watched the people come and take their seats in complete silence, their faces totally devoid of expression. Used as Heidi

50

and I were to our American hugs and noisy praises before services, this seemingly total lack of enthusiasm was unnerving.

After singing a number of songs in Arabic, Willie called me to the front and introduced me. As he introduced me, first in Arabic, then in French, I got my first inkling that I was going to be in for a distinctly new experience.

"And now . . ." Willie said in English, turning to face me, "you will bring the message. I will interpret for you."

I rose, cleared my throat nervously and began.

"Brothers and sisters . . ." I said, then paused. When I did so, Willie took that as his cue. As he had done when he had introduced me, he interpreted my first three words in Arabic, then in French. Trilingual preaching, I soon learned, was a slow, very difficult process. At least it was for me.

The flow of communication seemed awkward and jerky. In the middle of a sentence I would pause, as I normally did. But each time, Willie would take my pause as his cue, and he would pick it up and interpret into the other two languages. Though I have since become somewhat accustomed to this means of preaching, that first time was very difficult for me. It seemed to me that I was not communicating. Or that the people were receiving.

After a time, long before I would normally have completed my message, I summed it up and sat down. I felt defeated, as though my time had been wasted. I felt unaccountably depressed, a most unusual feeling for me.

During the closing hymn, my insightful wife leaned over and whispered to me. "What's wrong?"

"Everything I wanted to share seemed flat and

51

empty . . . it seems like I really bombed . . ."

"Didn't you minister the way the Lord directed you?" Heidi asked.

"Yes . . . to the best of my ability," I said.

She smiled reassuringly. "Then release it to the Lord. This is His business . . ."

I was thankful for my wife's belief in me, and gratefully accepted the encouragement she offered. At the close of the hymn, Willie spoke to the people for three or four minutes. Apparently he was asking questions of the congregation, because some people responded to him, some answering in Arabic, others in French.

I was oblivious to the content of this exchange, and was surprised when Willie turned and looked at me. "Brother Hershey, can you remain in Paris for a few days longer?"

"Stay in Paris?"

"Yes. We'd like for you to conduct meetings for us throughout the week. Can you do it?"

He caught me off guard. All the while I'd thought I'd failed—and now they wanted me to remain and teach them. Heidi and I had planned to leave the next morning to begin our sojourn in the Middle East. We conferred briefly, then I looked back at Willie.

"Yes . . . we'll change our flight arrangements and stay with you for three more days. And I'll conduct a special seminar on the principles of successful Christian Living . . ."

Willie smiled his thanks and quickly translated the news to the small congregation. They were obviously pleased.

The next three days passed quickly. In addition to my seminar, Heidi taught a class on praise and worship, then introduced Scripture songs. They loved these and learned them quickly. I learned that Willie's congregation was made up of Arabs from Egypt, Morocco, Algeria and a number of other Arab nations. But, it made no difference. Irregardless of the land of their birth, the hunger of these Arab brothers and sisters was universal. And it was wonderful to watch them learn to express themselves in times of worship and praise.

We learned to love a number of these Arab believers. I was impressed with one in particular. Ezat was born in Libya and had come to Europe to study. While there, he had been confronted with the Gospel and became a believer. I was foreign to the struggles and persecution faced by this young man.

"I don't personally know another believer in the entire country of Libya," Ezat told me. "And it's hard . . ."

He told me a story of bitter rejection by his family. "They won't communicate with me. They never answer my letters . . . but I believe that I will one day reach them for the Lord," he said.

Despite all these setbacks, though only in his early 20's, Ezat was preparing himself for the ministry. Ezat's vibrant love for the Lord Jesus is only one of thousands of such wonderful testimonies produced in the Middle East, and one that the whole world needs to hear. Ezat's life and testimony both challenged and humbled me.

Wednesday evening came, and with it the concluding session of the seminar. And just as believers do elsewhere in the world, they gathered for fellowship over food. It began as a time of rejoicing, but soon turned into something more significant. One man arose and spoke appreciatively of the ministry Heidi and I had shared with them, then he presented us with a beautiful poster signed by all the seminar participants.

It began when one Egyptian Arab asked, "How does one know for sure that he is saved?"

I hurriedly swallowed the bite of food I had in my mouth before I responded. That question was followed by another. Then another. Questions about doctrine. About the life and ministry of Jesus. About the interpretation of various passages of Scripture. About the issues they were facing as individuals and as a nation.

As I pondered and answered these questions that these people were struggling with, I glanced at Willie. He smiled and urged me to continue . . .

Again and again as I unravelled a difficult question and answered it from the Word, I saw the light of understanding come to a previously bewildered face. And I rejoiced with these brave and often persecuted people in the fact that "The name of the Lord is a strong tower: (and) the righteous runneth into it, and is safe" (Proverbs 18:10).

When the questioning finally ceased and Willie adjourned the meeting, I glanced at my watch. I was astonished to note that our time of fellowship had consumed more than four hours! A satisfying confirmation to "my Macadonian call."

5

THE MIDDLE EAST MAZE

"Ladies and gentlemen . . ." the loudspeaker boomed loudly in the crowded Cairo airport boarding lounge, "our flight to Nairobi will be delayed for an hour and a half. We are sorry for the inconvenience. Please make yourselves as comfortable as possible . . ."

Heidi and I just looked at each other. It was three-thirty A.M., and we had already been standing by to board "momentarily" for over an hour.

I shrugged. "Well, at least it won't be much longer."

Heidi sighed tiredly. "I'm going to try and rest." I helped move our bags so she could assume a more relaxed position. She leaned back and closed her eyes. But I was too keyed up to follow suit. Wearily my mind retraced our recent journeys. We had just spent three weeks roaming through the Mediterranean and Middle East: Greece, Cyprus, Israel and Egypt.

Each city and country had been spectacular in its own right in one way or another. Each had added materially to our growing store of information. And each had contributed to the insights we were gaining on ways to spearhead effective ministry in this troubled part of the world.

Originally I had thought that my understanding of how to share the Good News in the Middle East would have been enhanced by visiting key Christian leaders throughout the area. However, this had not always been the case. Instead, I thought, periphally aware of the airport hubub around me, we often found just the opposite to be true. And now as I struggled to put all the pieces together in my mind, I realized intellectually that my physical weariness was undoubtedly magnifying my conception of the enormous political, cultural and economic problems to be faced.

Not that my fatigue was creating the problems, because those problems were very real. But my utter weariness—compounded no doubt by the heat, the strange smells, the unfamiliar food, the continuous babble of languages that continually impinged me night and day—all of this was wearing me down. In fact, it was wearing us both down.

I thought about the times we had crossed security lines from one country to another, having in my possession names and addresses of key Middle East Arab and Jewish Christian leaders, along with what I believed to be my well thought-through detailed strategies of how to bring these leaders all together. Admittedly there were moments when I felt like I was sort of a "secret agent" for the Kingdom of God!

There had been those nightmarish times when I had imagined myself being arrested (for what reason I could only imagine) and detained. Perhaps for hours. Or even days. Such thoughts would cause my adrenalin to flow and my heartbeat to accelerate.

But now, sitting there in the crowded Cairo Airport, it seemed that my sleuthing had been in vain. Instead of clarifying my strategies to advance the Kingdom of God in these areas, just the opposite appeared to be the case. I seemed to have made a wrong turn somewhere. I no longer clearly saw the end from the beginning. My thinking had become muddled and blurred. I had come to a dead end. I was cornered . . . in a maze. A Middle East maze. And I couldn't find my way out.

My understanding of a maze was that its purpose was to confuse, to frustrate. With its dead ends, wrong turns, one-way roads, road-blocks, its confusing network of intricate turns and passages, the maze would bewilder the one who was unfortunate enough to find himself wandering therein.

If such was the state and purpose of a maze, this Middle East maze had most certainly achieved it's intended end on me.

As I mentally reviewed my situation, trying desperately to put it in perspective with the Word of God, it came to me again: the truth that God is not the Author of confusion. Therefore, there *had to be a way out* of this maze. And with the assistance of the Spirit of God, I must, *I would* find it.

"In all of Greece," my Greek friend had informed me, "there are no more than 7,000 born again believers! Fewer than in any other nation in Europe . . . and the cry of my heart is to see my people saved."

I thought of the proliferation of Greek Orthodoxy in that country, loudly professing religion, yet at the same time, evidencing a dearth of the glorious power of the Gospel. Truly "a dry and thirsty land where no water is."

To make matters worse, the socialist Greek govern-

THE WORLD IS WAITING

ment had made it a crime for anyone to proselyte a member of the Greek Orthodox Church. Which meant that it is illegal for anyone to publicly share the power of a changed life through Jesus Christ and invite people to commit themselves to His law of love. Especially if such a commitment might draw them away from the State Church.

I had learned that the Greek Orthodox Church wields tremendous power over 98 percent of the country's nine million citizens, the majority of whom automatically became members simply by being born in Greece. Yet only a mere two percent of the population attend church with any degree of regularity.

What a travesty, when one recalls the thrilling Book of Acts chronicle of the rapid spread of the Gospel throughout Greece as the Apostle Paul and his associates shared the Word. Personally I'll never forget the emotions that enveloped me when I first stood on Mars' Hill on the very spot where Paul first revealed to Athen's cynics the true identity of their "unknown god."

Oh, for a rerun of that long-ago "wildfire" acceptance of Jesus in the country of Greece! My heart burned within me with a great longing to assist my Greek brother in believing God for a mighty revival that would sweep through his beloved land.

Petrodollars spoke loudly to the Greece Heidi and I saw, as the Arab oil merchants' pervasive influence not only greatly influenced Greece's economy, but its religious life as well. The Arabs not only brought their money to Greece, but they also brought Islam as well, and I saw with my own eyes how Islam's religion and practices are steadily making themselves felt.

Cyprus had been similar to Greece in every respect. Although it is illegal for anyone to openly preach the

Gospel, the island nation is desperately in need of a spiritual awakening. The tension between Cypriots and Turks poses a constant threat to political stability. Turkey's invasion of Cyprus in the mid-70's is still a major hindrance to peace; and particularly since the Turks gained control of 40 percent of Cyprus at that time, Turkey is not at all interested in relinquishing her hold.

The maze's confusing network of dead ends seemed to become even more complex when we entered Israel.

The confusion was epitomized by the statement made by one of my evangelical brethren. "It's impossible to bring Jewish people into any sort of a Mid-East conference," he said.

"Why is that?" I asked, genuinely puzzled.

"Because of the division and hostility between Arabs and Jews," he told me. "During the early stages of any attempt for a Mid-East conciliation, you must bring only Arab leaders. A successful dialogue between them would in itself be tremendous progress . . ."

"But with no Jewish believers present?"

"Absolutely not," he said, "you've got to take one step at a time. Any Jewish presence in such a gathering would result in an explosive atmosphere in which nothing could be accomplished."

I listened intently, withholding comments or decisions. But, since it was our purpose to bring together believers from all of the Middle East countries, I still believed that there would be a way to do so. I was not at all opposed to hearing opposing points of view on the subject, but I was amazed at how often these views seemed to contradict each other.

A wrong turn in the maze, perhaps?

Another brother advised, "During any such conference as you are proposing, you must bring up the idea of the Palestinian homeland . . ."

"Isn't that inflammatory?" I asked.

He shook his head. "Perhaps, but you can't have a gathering of this nature and avoid such an issue."

Cautiously I said, "But you must realize that it is not our purpose to enter into a political dialogue. It is to generate fellowship around God's Word . . . and to focus on the risen Lord."

As I listened to these many differing opinions, I could see very clearly just how difficult it is for people to set aside their differences and to be able to enter into His presence. To simply worship the Lord together. Despite all these maze-like ideas I was hearing, I was becoming even more firmly convinced of the rightness of my conviction that if people of any ethnic background could only worship the Lord together that their differences would dissipate.

It must be so, I reasoned, remembering the Psalmist's theme as recorded in Psalm 133. "Behold, how good and how pleasant it is for brethren to dwell together in unity! It is like the precious ointment upon the head . . ."

As I meditated upon these anointed words, I realized again that this must be my approach if I was to succeed in helping to pull God's people together, either in the Middle East or elsewhere in the world, where hostility and hatred and pride were at work to alienate one part of the Body with another.

Perhaps it was while in Israel that this concept was even more forcibly brought to my attention. Israel: the land and the people that God had chosen as special. It was to these people that God had specifically declared, "I the Lord have called thee in righteousness, and will hold thine hand, and will keep thee, and give thee for a covenant of the people, *for a light of the Gentiles . . .*" (Isaiah 42:7).

Yet, paradoxically, even amongst these chosen people, especially the Orthodox, there appeared to be greater variance than with the others, the "less" spiritual Jews. I found myself struggling to understand.

While in Jerusalem, Heidi and I spent a most unforgetable hour. It was late one Friday afternoon, and we were to meet a Messianic Jewish believer who was on patrol duty. An Israeli Army officer was to lead us to our rendezvous. We had known that the Jewish Shabbat or Sabbath began at sundown Friday and ended when the first star appeared the following evening. During this 24-hour period, all work ceased. Families enjoyed their special Shabbat meal together, then the men made their way to synagogue to study Torah and to pray.

It was not yet sundown when the officer began leading us up what seemed an interminably long stairway that led to the rooftop where our friend was patrolling. Midway on our journey it became necessary for us to pass through a very small Jewish home in order for us to reach the rooftop.

The officer unceremoniously pushed open the door and led us through the tiny one-room dwelling. I was aware of the dark-clothed figure of a man, seated facing the eastern wall of his home. Though I felt discomfort as Heidi and I followed the officer through the room, I was also very curious.

Neither the officer nor the resident spoke, and I gathered that this "intrusion" must of necessity be a regular occurrence since it was apparently the only access to this section of the city's rooftops.

I quickly glanced around the sparsely-furnished

room. To me it evidenced deep poverty. The only furniture seemed to be a small bed that was shoved against one wall. An old refrigerator and a wooden table with two benches occupied the center of the room.

During those few seconds in which we moved through this Jewish man's domain, my eyes were drawn again to the lone figure against the wall. He was wearing a traditional kepah or skull-cap of the Orthodox male, and a tallit or prayer shawl was draped around his shoulders. I could hear him speaking or chanting in a subdued monotone, while bobbing his upper torso back and forth. I realized I was witnessing a Jewish man in the midst of his Shabbat prayers.

When we had passed through the room and were again ascending the endless steps, Heidi and I looked at each other. "He must be used to these interruptions," I said.

She smiled somewhat embarrassedly. "It wouldn't be the most pleasant way to live."

A minute later we reached the rooftop, a vantage point from which we had a panoramic view of Jerusalem and the Western or so-called "Wailing Wall." It was a sight I shall long remember. Dusk was rapidly descending, and in the semidarkness we could make out hundreds of Jewish people approaching the Wall to say their Shabbat prayers.

I must have gasped at the entrancing sight.

The officer smiled understandingly. "Friday nights are very spectacular from here," he said. "They are times of happiness and joy. After the prayers you will see hundreds joining these who are already here for singing and dancing. Shabbats are always very special occasions."

We became aware of another person with us, and I realized it was the Messianic Jew we had come to meet. Though our new friend appeared to be nearing the half-century mark, he carried himself with a youthful dignity and self assurance that was very appealing. And one that bespoke itself of something else, a spirit of peace. That was it: the epitome of shalom, the Sabbath peace.

During our time upon the rooftop I could not but notice the security precautions being observed below us. Armed soldiers checked each person who entered the large open area facing the Western Wall.

"Why?" I asked.

"It's necessary," he explained, "because of the frequent threats by Arab terrorists. We dare not relax our vigilance for a single moment." He told us that this eternal vigilance made it necessary for every Israeli to serve a month each year in the armed forces until he reached the age of 55.

We were silent for a few minutes as we watched the crowds gather below us. Then I asked my Messianic friend a question that had been burning within me since I reached Israel.

"What move of God is taking place among the Orthodox Jews?"

"It's quite interesting," he began. "Recently there's been a noticeable surge of interest in the worship of God. I guess you could say that revival is now taking place amongst the Orthodox."

"Revival . . ." I said, savoring the word. "That's tremendous. Does this mean that the Orthodox Jews are actually beginning to recognize Jesus as their Messiah?"

He shook his head. "Not really. Many of them claim to have experienced a 'new birth,' but what they mean by that is a time of deep personal repentance and a resurgence of stricter observance of Jewish Law. It's not the recognition of Jesus as the Messiah. Nevertheless, great numbers of Jews are seeking the living God."

We spent about an hour with our friend on the rooftop: discussing the plight of the Jewish nation as well as that of the Messianic Jews in Israel. We learned that even though the Messianic Jewish community is growing, their acceptance by the Jewish community is minimal at most.

I said, "Then there's still much work to be done."

"Yes," he responded, "much work."

Heidi and I had much to think about as we followed our new friends down the stairs, through the tiny apartment, and onto the streets. That hour or so had resulted in much deeper insight and understanding concerning our Jewish brothers. I thanked the Lord for leading us to this place.

I broke the silence in which we walked for a few minutes. "What a day, Heidi. What a day . . ." My wife nodded in agreement. Deep in our own thoughts, she and I spoke little as we made our way to our room for the night.

At the time we were in Israel, David, my younger brother was a resident student in Jerusalem. His purpose was to master the Hebrew language and to gain a better understanding of the Jewish people and their culture. During our times together, David and his friends spent many hours with us, discussing the distinctions and contradictions of Jewish Orthodoxy.

David told me of his writing a paper on the subject of the Arab/Israeli conflict for one of his classes in which he was to not only define the problem, but also suggest a solution. I was rather intrigued with his analysis of the problem, but even more so with his solution, which he aptly wrapped up in his closing line. It was: "Love your neighbor as yourself . . . if you can."

Simplistic? Perhaps. But probably more practical than those posed by many self-styled international peace negotiators.

In Galilee, Heidi and I visited an Arab Christian pastor who was very concerned about the persecution suffered by Messianic believers at the hands of Orthodox Jews. He informed us that there are approximately twenty-five Messianic Jewish synagogues, having a total of about 2,000 believers in all of Israel.

This dear Arab brother, who possessed a deep heart's desire to see Arabs and Jews fellowshipping, told me of the wonderful times he had experienced when he and his church invited neighboring Messianic brothers to worship with them in their church. This pastor was one of the few I met who was actually working out a practical solution to the complex problem, despite the obstacles that stood in the way.

Why were there so few producing results to these spiritual problems? I asked myself. And why was this brother one of the very few who was seeing peaceful results to the complex spiritual problems in Jerusalem and throughout Israel?

The answer, I thought, might be because this pastor seems to truly believe—as few others seem to believe—that God, if given the opportunity, could and would bring a cessation to hostilities, and with that, a lasting peace.

From Israel, Heidi and had flown directly to Cairo, where we were met with immediate, staggering personal problems. First, we learned that we must purchase entrance visas at the price of $150 each.

(Nobody had apprised us of this expense.) Next, even as as we were haggling with government officials over those visas, we saw a man walking out of the airport with our luggage!

When we had finally solved the visa problem and retrieved our luggage, we exited the airport only to have our now sensibilities assaulted by the ear-splitting and mind-shattering noise caused by hundreds of Egyptians shouting at the top of their voices. Not understanding the situation, we assumed they were shouting at us.

Heidi's face was white with fear. "What shall we do?"

"Just look straight ahead and ignore them," I said.

At that point I wished I'd taken time to arrange for someone to meet us. But I realized that would have been impossible, for our itinerary had been changed at the last moment, and this had been the only available flight to Cairo.

Outside the airport mall we were apalled to see literally thousands of people sleeping on the ground. Then it occurred to me that this was the time of the year for the faithful Moslems to make their annual pilgrimage to Mecca.

The very air was charged. What was it? I wondered. Then, I knew. It was oppression. Oppression so heavy and thick that it pervaded the very air we breathed. We found ourselves feeling almost claustrophobic and we prayed that God would surround us to protect us.

Finally, after an eternity of waiting, I managed to hail a cab. Minutes later we gratefully slammed our hotel door behind us and sank wearily upon our bed.

Before I closed my eyes to rest, the words of an Egyptian pastor I had met in England popped into my mind. "Many believers in Egypt are frightened for their lives," he said. "They are all suffering heavy persecution and discrimination . . ."

I was to think of those words many times during the following forty eight hours as I tried in vain to make contact with Egyptian believers. Though I spent hours at a time on the phone, it seemed that everything I did was in vain. I felt as though Satan himself had launched an all-out attack against me personally and the mission I had come here to accomplish.

During our two days in Cairo, as far as we could determine, we accomplished absolutely nothing that we had set out to do. Zero. Bombed out.

"Ladies and gentlemen . . ." the announcement began.

I was abruptly jolted from my reveries and reflections. I could scarcely make out the garbled words, but I heard enough. I shook Heidi. "It's time to board!" I shouted. "The plane for Nairobi just arrived! Let's get aboard."

Heidi quickly roused herself and grabbed her bags. We wanted nothing more than to leave Cairo. The sooner the better. Not until we had pushed and shoved ourselves and our luggage on board and the heavily-loaded plane was in the air did we relax.

"The maze . . ." I said to Heidi.

"The what?" she asked. "What did you say?"

"It's the maze. The Middle East maze. We're certainly having a time finding our way through it . . ."

I pushed the button and reclined my seat. "But I'm very glad that Jesus knows the way through . . ."

A FAMINE IN THE LAND

Before ministering in Malawi, Heidi and I had been involved in similar evangelistic efforts in Kenya. And though God had done wondrous things among us there, I had never before experienced such a spontaneous response to Jesus' message: "Come unto Me."

I caught my breath at the sight.

Hopeful faces uplifted, their hands imploringly extended, scores of my Malawi listeners were now jammed so tightly around me that I could scarcely move or breathe.

What had I done, what did I say that had so instantaneously ignited them into action?

Quickly I remembered. All I had done was to extend my opened arms toward them and say words that I have said, dozens of times in other contexts—"If you want to renounce your sins and your old ways . . . if you want to experience forgiveness and peace . . . come to Jesus. Not tomorrow. Come to Him *now*!"

The words had hardly left my mouth when a third or more of the crowd rushed toward me with one accord. Some were weeping and crying aloud. Others, faces strained with emotion, merely pressed toward me with strong resolve. Within mere seconds I found myself inextricably thronged by a mass of humanity!

Those simple words had been the catalyst that had served to activate the action I now witnessed. It was the move of the Holy Spirit as I spoke those words that gave the impetus and motivated them, almost as one person, to leap to their feets and fling themselves at me.

As evangelists, Heidi and I were participating in a citywide campaign designed to present the Gospel to the total populace of Malawi's then capital city of Blantyre. Along with a group of African ministers we were preaching and teaching at all hours, in every available location, endeavoring to do, as our slogan read, reach the city of "Blantyre for Jesus."

This noon hour I had been preaching to a crowd of workers in a textile factory during their lunch break. Of the approximately 2,000 employees, over 300 had chosen to listen to me preach as they ate their lunch. At the close of my brief message, I had invited my hearers to come to Jesus.

And they had done so. They had come running to Jesus. Running! Eager to shed their old ways and their old life! Eager to experience His new life and to be clothed in His righteousness.

My heart went out to them. Though Malawi is a beautiful country, the people and nation are poverty stricken. And as I beheld the faces that surrounded me, I saw two kinds of hunger written on them. I thought of the Prophet Amos' words: "Behold, the days come, saith the Lord God, that I will send a famine in the land, not a famine of bread, nor a thirst for water, but of hearing the words of the Lord" (Amos 8:11).

The thin, pinched faces and emaciated bodies before me spoke loudly of their need for food. But the hunger expressed in their eyes spoke even more eloquently of the greater famine. I was witnessing the fulfilment of the Prophet's words.

There was a famine in this land!

Though the people were hungry . . . and though Malawi's lack of water was crucial, the true famine that was destroying the real life of these people had to do with the needs of the spirit.

It was their famine of the Word of the Lord.

Later that day when I returned to our mission headquarters, I could tell immediately that Heidi's experience had paralleled mine. She was beaming.

"What happened?" I asked.

In her enthusiasm to relate her story, Heidi's words tumbled over each other, overlapped and ran together. "Well, as you know, my assignment was to go with Chris to preach at a bus stop . . . just an ordinary bus stop, where there's usually a good crowd of people waiting for their bus . . ."

She paused and I nodded.

"Well, we sang a few songs. And when we had the attention of a hundred or so people, I began giving my testimony through an interpreter."

"Did they listen to you?" I asked.

"Yes. There was total silence while I spoke."

"Then what?"

"Then Chris simply explained what I meant when I invited them to be born again. He defined in their language and context what it would mean to have that sort of intimate fellowship with God. Then he asked if anybody wanted to have that experience?"

"And . . ." I prodded.

Heidi's eyes were alive with excitement. "And they all responded."

"At first I was stunned. So was Chris. And we weren't sure they understood. So we tried again. This time we asked everyone who was *really serious* about changing his ways and living for the Lord *to kneel down* while we prayed for them."

"Did some of them do it?" I asked.

"Yes. They all did. All of them got down on their knees in the rough gravel at the bus stop. And they all prayed with us to be born again, to be forgiven of their sins . . ."

Afterwards, Heidi told me, some of the people stayed longer to be individually prayed for and counseled with. "It's remarkable!" I said, then related my own experience.

Clearly, there was indeed a famine in this land. And our part to play in alleviating that famine was to feed the people by serving them large portions of the Bread of Life. We went to bed that night full of anticipation for what God would do during the remainder of our two-week "Blantyre for Jesus" campaign.

I was learning something very important about evangelism: God has special times and seasons for the planting, the watering *and* the harvesting of His Word. The Apostle Paul stated it well when he wrote to the Corinthian Church, "I have planted, Apollos watered; but God gave the increase" (I Corinthians 3:6). It's the Genesis Principle.

Even though there is famine in a land or among a people, no single person has it within his power to generate a harvest *unless* there has already been a time of planting. And a time of watering. And, finally, the time for harvest. Over a century ago David Livingstone had recognized the need and had planted the Word of God in Africa. And during the intervening years, scores of missionaries and preachers had watered that Word.

And now, Heidi and I, and the other African ministers were God's instruments for harvest.

Even though we were aware of the tremendous famine of the Word of God in Europe, the Middle East and other countries of Africa, we hadn't personally witnessed times of harvest in those places as we were presently witnessing in Malawi. The reason: in Malawi the previous, preliminary work had been accomplished. The seeds had been watered. They had sprouted and the planting had matured. And the time for harvesting had arrived.

We were the fortunate ones who were witnessing the harvest.

In Europe, the Middle East, and other countries in Africa, the cycle apparently had not yet run its full course.

The time for Malawi was *now*. And we were taking full advantage of that knowledge. The hunger was everywhere, amongst every level and stratum of society. Amongst the educated and the ignorant. Among the rich and the poor. Among the churched and the unchurched. Among adherents of many religions . . .

Christians were getting awakened and revived; while Buddhists, Hindus, Muslims and others, were accepting Jesus as Lord!

I had always been under the impression that it would be long, difficult and tedious work to labor among people of other cultures and to lead them to Jesus. Perhaps in many, even most cases this would be true. But when it is God's harvest time, and when

73

there is a supernatural moving of God's Holy Spirit, anything can happen. And here in Malawi, I was experiencing this omnipotent dimension of God's power as it had never been my privilege before.

And it was thrilling!

We were seeing God answer prayers in behalf of these famine-bound people in ways that were beyond our comprehension. Had we even tried to do so, we could not have "set up" circumstances so perfectly as we were presently witnessing our Father do as we were praying and reaching out with His message.

This was most certainly so in the case of our friend Bambo Jambo. Actually, that wasn't his real name, which was so unpronounceable to the American tongue that by common consent we all settled upon the less difficult Bambo Jambo. He understood and good naturedly accepted the nickname.

Bambo Jambo assisted Heidi and me in caring for the little cottage in which we and three others lived while in Malawi. He was not a Christian, and as we discussed this matter with him, Bambo Jambo responded, "I have been a Muslim all of my life. I have very carefully studied the Koran and the teachings of Mohammed."

I heard him out and made no attempt to debate him. Instead, I told him the reason for our team being in Malawi. I told him that Jesus loved him and that He wanted to bless him and his family. Then I gave him a New Testament.

Bambo Jambo thanked me for the New Testament. "I will read it when I have time," he promised.

All five residents of our cottage made it a point to pray daily for Bambo Jambo. Nevertheless, after my discussion with the man, though Bambo Jambo was friendly and gracious, he made it clear to us all that he had no interest in further dialogues about Jesus.

One morning when Bambo Jambo came to the cottage, he looked very upset. I asked him why. He said, "My little child was taken to the hospital this morning . . ."

"What was the reason?"

"The doctor thinks it's some kind of poison . . ." He wrung his hands in despair.

I told him, "Bambo Jambo, my friends and I are going to ask God to totally heal your little boy."

He thanked me and seemed somewhat relieved as he went on about his work. The five of us went to prayer immediately. We prayed that God would not only heal Bambo Jambo's son, but that through this healing Bambo Jambo would know that Jesus is alive and that He cared for him and his family in a personal way.

The next morning Bambo Jambo bounced into our little cottage with a beaming face. "My son is okay!" he said. "He is fine. He was released from the hospital yesterday afternoon. And the doctors can't find anything wrong with him."

I shook his hand and said, "Praise the Lord for his goodness."

The day Heidi and I were leaving, we spoke with Bambo Jambo once again about Jesus. "I have started reading the materials you gave me," he said.

"Very good," I said, "but have you thought any more about asking Jesus to come into your heart and to forgive you of your sins? You know by now that He loves you very much and wants to let you participate in His life."

Bambo Jambo hesitated for a moment before answering. "I was thinking that maybe in about a year or so I will change my religion . . ."

I spoke gently, but kindly, "Bambo Jambo, why not do it now, and let Jesus' love and peace fill you now?"

With hardly any hesitation, Bambo Jambo smiled and said, "Okay. I think now is the time."

As Heidi and I prayed with Bambo Jambo that day, he made a simple transaction with God, and made Jesus Christ his Lord. Bambo Jambo's transaction with the God was only one of many we were privileged to participate in during our time in Malawi.

Again and again we saw God demonstrate His power and love in such tangible ways that the people didn't resist. They simply opened their hearts to Him and responded to His call. Undoubtedly we were in the midst of a revival.

Time and again, the words of the chorus I learned as a child came to me during those days, words that were certainly illustrating what we were seeing. "Only believe. Only believe. All things are possible, only believe . . ."

In this dry and thirsty land, were were seeing the impossible being accomplished daily: by the simple expedient of believing.

I was learning that there is no room for unbelief in God's work. And that in order to flow with God in evangelism during times of revival and the powerful moves of His Holy Spirit, unbelief is totally out of place. For unbelief will effectively quench the power of God and prevents the operation of His mighty works of power. It was because of such unbelief that Jesus was unable to do mighty works in Nazareth. (Matthew 13:58)

And it was while we were ministering in Malawi, that I was to experience the power of belief in a most amazing way.

It came about as I was assisting Stephen, one of our African brothers, in an open air campaign. Before I had ministered in music, I gave a brief word of exhortation, encouraging people to expect God to meet their every possible need—". . . *this very night*— as the Word was being proclaimed. Then I sat down and prayed that God would accomplish that very thing.

After Stephen had delivered a dynamic message, he made a most surprising announcement.

"If there is anyone here tonight with a special need in his life, particularly sickness in his body, line up over here . . ."

I watched the people rise from their seats and move toward the designated spot.

At Stephen's next words I froze.

"Now," he said, "this young American evangelist will pray for you . . . *and God will heal you!*"

To say that I was shocked would be a gross understatement. Stephen and I had known each other for some time. We had met and ministered together in the United States. I don't personally know any man who is more committed to Christ and His ministry and who carries any more of a burden to see the Gospel prevail than Stephen. Nor do I know a man who is more sensitive to the leading of the Holy Spirit.

Therefore, I knew that for Stephen to select me to pray for the sick and needy meant that God had directed him to do so. But when I moved to the designated area of the large open field and noted the long line of people for whom I was to pray, I gasped. There seemed to be no end to it.

One by one they came—just as they had come to Jesus. And, one by one, as I laid my hands on them in Jesus' name, their manifold symptoms departed.

Often instantly! Some came limping and left leaping. Pain disappeared. Fear departed. Peace came and ruled.

And they praised God for His mercy, His peace, His healing power! I had never seen anything like this, and I thanked God that He was seeing fit to use me as His instrument.

One man admitted to me through the interpreter, "I have the disease that women give."

By the way he described his symptoms, I realized the young man was afflicted with a serious venereal disease. "I have just committed my life to Jesus," he told me, "and I want you to pray that the Lord will heal my body." After I prayed for him, he too, departed joyfully, running and leaping and praising God.

Stephen asked me to preach the following night. At the conclusion of my short message I was grateful to see scores of people come forward to make Jesus their Lord. This time I felt prompted to pray for the sick once again, and a large number lined up, expecting to receive God's healing touch upon their bodies and in their lives.

Among those in the line was a man who asked, "Do you remember me?"

"I'm sorry," I said, "I remember you, but there have been so many people that I can't remember your name."

My interpreter reminded me, "This is the young man you prayed for last night to be healed of a venereal disease."

"Yes," the young man said eagerly, "yes, I'm the one. And when I went home, I undressed and looked at myself . . . and I was healed! My body was perfectly normal! And even the part of my body that was rotting was already restored."

"Glory to God!" I said.

"Now I want everything God has for me," he said. "I want to live by the power of God. Will you pray for me that I will be filled with God's Holy Spirit?"

"Of course," I said, and took a few minutes to explain to my new friend how this power could become a reality in his life. Afterwards he again left singing praises to God.

God honors such belief. He has shown me that it *is possible* for God's people to win the world for Jesus Christ through believers who will pray in belief and then act upon their faith.

Those days and nights in Blantyre were long and strenuous. But they were glorious. There were times when we were nearly overcome with physical weariness, but each time as we waited on the Lord in preparation for ministry, our strength was renewed. And each time Heidi and I and the others preached or taught or shared the precious truths from His Word, that vitalized Word bore fruit and lives were changed.

I learned much in those days in Blantyre working with my African brothers. Laboring in love with them I learned principles that will doubtless stand me in good stead throughout my life. And at the same time, reading and rereading the anointed words of the Apostle Paul, especially his Letter to the Colossians, I gained insights I shall never forget.

I learned that God's people must work together in love. They must humbly cooperate with each other without criticism or fault finding, being instruments of blessing, willing to serve others as though that service was being personally rendered unto Jesus.

Such mutuality in service must be directed by and patterned after the total integrity of God's Word, including the sometimes painful declaration of the whole counsel of God.

There were times in Blantyre when the hours were long and the ministry assignments were difficult. But as we each allowed God's Spirit to direct us through His Word we became so firmly welded together in love that Satan's efforts to destroy our unity were ineffective.

Our times of prayer, when we, separately or together, spent much time with our Master, became times of power as we joined our spirits with His Spirit, thus making it possible for all of us to "stand perfect and complete in all the will of God" (Colossians 4:12).

We had worked so intensely with each other during these weeks that when the time came for us to depart, it was not easy for us to leave our brothers and sisters. A number of local ministers, teachers and evangelists would be remaining behind to consolidate and conserve the results of our combined efforts.

Before we departed, we prayed for each other. We prayed that God would continue to revive this dry and thirsty land. We prayed that our visions would continue to expand. We prayed that our eyes would continually be opened to new needs, to new opportunities, and that our service to God would expand accordingly.

During those last minutes together, I looked around the room, allowing my eyes to rest for a few moments on each person. I was humbled as I did so. Hardly a person present owned a decent suit or change of clothing. Many of them habitually went to bed hungry much of the time. Only a few of them possessed even a bicycle, much less a more sophisticated means of transportation. Many of them would walk miles each day to minister God's Word.

Yet there was a light in their eyes, an expression of joy upon their faces, a spring in their steps that belied their physical hunger and weariness. Like Jesus at the well, they had eaten meat the world knew not off. As with the Master, their "meat was to do the will of their Father in heaven."

I heard the report. "Brothers and sisters, during these weeks more than 8,000 people have made personal commitments to follow Jesus Christ!"

Eight thousand people!

We praised God together and sang again our theme song, "Africa Belongs to God."

Heidi and I were silent a long time after we left. It *is true* Africa *does* belong to God. Praise God! He is Lord.

7

SOUTH AFRICA

Contentedly I closed my eyes. All around me I could
hear the happy noises of the birds and the refreshing
sound of falling water. I was aware of Heidi as she,
too, stretched out full length beside me in the balmy
sunlight.

"This must be something like the Garden of Eden,"
I said dreamily. "All of this greenery . . . the flowers,
trees . . . the waterfalls . . ."

For the first time in months of continuous travel
Heidi and I now had a place all to ourselves. And
after traipsing across half of Europe and the Mediterranean, we had finally located ourselves in a beautiful
retreat center where we could unpack and set up
housekeeping for a short period of time. This lovely
little villa, a short commute from Durban, South Africa, had been generously provided for us by Michael
Cassidy and African Enterprise for the specific purpose of resting and regaining our strength in preparation for the strenuous service that yet lay before us.
Though we both appreciated the thoughtfulness of
this cottage, Heidi was nearly beside herself with joy.

Our planned ministry for the next few months would be conducted from this base of operations.

As I lazed half-dozing in the sun, I mentally reviewed our situation. Though I had heard much of the problems of South Africa, this is the very first time I'd ever personally visited this great country, and quite frankly I had very little idea of what I could or should expect. What would it be like, I wondered, to be involved in evangelism in a country that was fractured by so many divisive forces, including the pervasive spectre of apartheid?

I knew this policy could not but have a drastic effect upon our earnest efforts to spread the Gospel. With its rigid segregation of whites from blacks, blacks from coloreds, and Indians from all the rest, it could not be otherwise. Though the definitions of apartheid varied, the bottom line, I knew, was minority rule by the European whites—and the strictest possible kind of segregation, including political and economic discrimination against all non-European groups.

The inevitable result, of course, was hatred and hostility such as I had never seen.

Though I had lived in Southern United States, I realized that in my brief lifetime I had never witnessed any discrimination such as I would now be involved in. And I'll have to admit that I was a little uncertain of the prospect.

However, I would not be thrust into this alone. I would be accompanied and tutored by David, an articulate and powerful Indian evangelist of many years' experience. David and I were old friends. Several years before, he and I had met in the United States, where, in a reversed role, I had accompanied and guided him on a ministry tour in my own country.

And I shall never forget the night, after a long day of travel and ministry, when we relaxed in a hotel room in San Francisco. He had kicked off his shoes, put his feet on the bed and leaned back. I had done the same. After several moments of relaxed, friendly silence, he had opened his eyes and spoken.

"Keith, you need a wife."

I was startled. "A wife . . .?"

"Yes. A wife. If you're going to be effective in the ministry, especially in the ministry of itinerant evangelism, you will very definitely need a wife."

It was as though he had been reading my mind. I knew he was right, and I had thought about the matter for some months. But as yet, the right young woman had not appeared on the matrimonial horizon. I answered slowly. "Yes . . . David, you are right. I do need a wife . . . and I have been praying for just the right one . . ."

"Then let's pray together for one," he said. Without hesitation, he dropped down on his knees and besought the Lord for "just the right woman for my brother. One who will love him and care for him. One who will believe in his vision and support his ministry efforts . . ."

I had been very touched by his earnest prayer. And as we arose from our knees, I quipped, "David, as soon as the answer to this prayer is manifested, I'll bring my bride to Africa with me to preach the Gospel . . ."

True to form, David's prayer had been heard. Several years after our prayer time together, Heidi and I were wed in a lovely Christmas celebration. And now we were happily engaged in the work the Lord had laid upon my heart. Furthermore, I was teamed up to preach the Gospel with the very man who had been instrumental in bringing this blessing to pass.

Little had I known then just how much David's life and mine—and now the life of the lovely wife he had helped me pray for—would be entwined in international evangelism. Neither could I have known at that time just how much I would learn from this spiritual giant of both the life of faith as well as the techniques and principles of evangelism. Among those principles he was to teach me was that when one is being led of the Holy Spirit, no obstacle can stand in the way of success, and no evil can prevail.

South Africa is one of the most beautiful and yet one of the most paradoxical places in the world. South Africa's travel folders tout it as being "a microcosm of the world." Whatever that means, much of it is true: South Africa is blessed with almost unlimited resources of natural beauty and mineral resource—all of which the world seeks.

Sadly though, as I was to learn more and more first hand, South Africa is also cursed with the unbearable discrimination and oppression of its peoples—which the world cannot tolerate.

David was to teach me much about all of this.

"Come with me, beloved Brother Keith and Sister Heidi," he said to us one day after we had recouped our sagging energies, "and let's go down to The Tavern for a time of prayer . . ."

"The *tavern*, David?" I asked. "What's the tavern?"

He smiled at my discomfiture. "Oh . . . The Tavern's where I go to pray and counsel. It's also where I go to preach and evangelize . . ."

"But *tavern* . . . doesn't that have a negative connotation?"

"Not really," he said, flashing his beautiful white teeth. "I suppose it used to be a tavern before some

Christian businessmen purchased it and made it available for me. Come. You'll see."

Heidi and I were to learn that The Tavern was used in the community as a place of redemption, a place where the "wine of the Holy Spirit" flows freely. A place where one can slake the deepest thirsts known to mankind. And a place where "whosoever will" may come for guidance, fellowship and peace.

It was while praying in The Tavern that David and I often received our "marching orders" from the Lord. And it was from this place where we launched our evangelistic efforts into various areas of this region in South Africa. And it was in this place where, time and again we saw God move in the lives of those who came to The Tavern to receive release from the suffering of their stressed lives. And from this place that those who came seldom went away empty-handed or empty-hearted.

Much of our ministry in South Africa was among the Indian populace, a high percentage of whom were Hindus by faith. How wonderful it was to repeatedly see the Spirit of the Living God in action as He penetrated the blinded hearts of those hearers and produced in them a vibrant Christian faith.

I well remember one night in particular when I counted about 85 people in the meeting, most of them Indian. Yet when the invitation was given, all but 5 came forward to pray.

In my mind is a cameo portrait of one of them, a tiny Indian girl who stumbled forward during the altar call, her eyes nearly blinded by tears. "What's the trouble?" Heidi asked her.

"I want to be forgiven," the child said.

What transpired was a sight I will long remember: of my lovely, light-skinned wife with her arm around the dark-skinned little girl. And as they prayed their tears flowed together.

On another occasion I was present when Heidi ministered at the first service of what was to become a ladies' prayer group. For this initial meeting the women were encouraged to invite their husbands, so there were nearly as many men present in the small rural church as there were women. After Heidi finished speaking, I stood with her as she invited people to come forward for prayer, and a number of them responded.

One couple came together. Brokenly they told of their plans to dissolve their marriage and break up their home. Somehow they had come to this meeting together. And as Heidi had spoken, God had spoken too, and had shown them that His love could heal even their shattered relationship, and renew in them the love they once had for one another. Each seemed to be eager to accept the blame for the failure of their marriage.

"I'm so very sorry . . ." the woman said as tears streamed down her face. "I have done so many wrong things . . ."

He broke in. "I don't know why I acted as I did," he said, "except that I wasn't doing things God's way. And now I want to try again . . . and this time do it God's way."

Ignoring us, the couple wept and confessed to each other. Heidi and I realized we weren't needed. This was God's business and this man and this woman were in His presence. So we did nothing. And as the couple opened their hearts to each other and to Him, God began the healing of the breach.

The woman looked at me. "It's wonderful . . . wonderful what God has done for us . . ." Then, rather shyly, looking first at her husband then at me, she asked, "We need to renew our marriage vows . . . would you . . .?"

Her husband picked it up. "Yes. Yes . . . that's what we both want. Will you reunite us in marriage?"

I smiled. "Of course. I'll be happy to do that. When shall we do it?"

"Right now," he said. "There's not need to wait. Let's do it now."

She nodded happily, unable to speak.

He turned to me. "We're ready right now."

"Then so am I," I said. So the meeting closed with me helping them recommit their lives to the Lord, and their reunited marriage into His leadership. It was a memorable day for us all.

Reflecting upon the day's events, I realized we had been privileged to witness a special principle of God's at work. "It's wonderful," I told Heidi, "that when you really have a revelation of the extent and the power of God's love, that nothing can separate you from that love . . ."

She agreed, adding, "Nor can any of His children be torn from each other . . ."

"That's right. Then, somehow, our petty little differences will simply disappear in the light of His presence. And when that happens we suddenly discover that what we had thought was a problem really isn't a problem at all. It has just sort of melted away when it was examined under the microscope of His Word."

At one of our campmeetings in South Africa, Heidi and I rather nervously observed an all-black congregation gather for the service. We could tell by the way they were pointing and staring at us that some of them were as apprehensive as we were.

Our African host seemed to sense our feelings. He

leaned toward me and cleared his throat. "Brother Keith, you don't know how rare white people are around here . . ."

"What do you mean?" I asked.

"Well, counting you and Heidi, you two are only the fourth white people that many of these folks have heard minister."

"Really? That surprises me."

"You've got to remember that this is an African township," our host said, "and hardly any white folks ever come here."

We had been invited to preach at the annual camp-meeting held in this township, which drew believers from all over South Africa, an invitation we quickly accepted. Though we had ministered numerous times amongst African nations, this would be our first in an all-black township. We had been advised by some that we should obtain a government permit before entering a black township. And now, as I surveyed the auditorium, I wondered with some apprehension if I shouldn't have done so.

Heidi whispered to me, "I wonder what they're thinking of us?"

"They probably think we represent exactly what the government represents," I told her, noting the curious, though not unfriendly sea of faces. But I knew in my heart that God had sent us here, and that God had assured me of my ordination unto the nations, so I decided to move with confidence, a confidence I was far from feeling. The time came for me to minister, and I was introduced to the congregation.

I had a flash of inspiration and made a bold move.

"My brother and I are just alike," I began, throwing my arm around the shoulder of my black African interpreter.

I could see some people stiffen. But before they had time to react, I went on. "The Bible teaches us that the *real me* and the *real you* are deeper than the skin. They are inside of us . . ."

No response from the congregation.

"All of us are spirits," I went on. "We possess souls and we are housed in bodies. Now listen very carefully, my friends. Our bodies may look different on the outside. But *on the inside my brother and I are just alike!*"

I paused for emphasis. Still no visible response, though the tension seemed to relax somewhat.

"Both my brother and I are just alike," I said slowly. "We have both made Jesus Christ the Lord of our lives. And we are both new creatures. New creations . . ."

Getting my point across through an interpreter was slow and tedious, and I was eager for the punch line.

"God is also a Spirit, Jesus told us, and we must worship Him in spirit and in truth . . ."

Here and there I noticed a man or woman relax their shoulders and lean back in their seats. A few smiled and nodded in agreement with my last words.

"Friends," I continued, "the *only difference* between my brother and myself . . ." (I indicated my interpreter again), ". . . is that his house is one color and mine is another. But that doesn't matter. Because inside *we are exactly the same*—created in the image of God!"

The response was instantaneous. That last sentence seemed to release the tension completely. As one person the congregation began laughing and applauding and praising God.

From that moment of release, the listeners readily received what the Lord had given me to share with them. And at the close of the service, when I gave the invitation, the response of these people was no different than than of any other village, city or township: they arose to their feet and moved toward God—to receive pardon . . . or cleansing . . . or healing . . . or the empowering of the Holy Spirit.

It was shortly after this event that I received a personal word from the Lord that has left a lasting impression my life. I was studying the Word, and had paused to meditate or think deeply about the Scripture I'd been considering.

I was fully awake and not the least bit drowsy at the time, when it seemed that the Lord was speaking directly to me by impressing something upon my mind. I heard His voice saying, "You have been chosen to assist in winning the world."

The words were unmistakable. I knew I had not heard audible words, but rather the words seemed to have been spoken from inside of me. I paused, hoping to hear more. But that was all I heard: "You have been chosen to assist in winning the world."

The thought was new to me. And at that time I couldn't remember having read it before. Using my concordance, I learned that God had spoken almost these identical words when He called Jeremiah. "I ordained thee a prophet unto the nations," He said (Jeremiah 1:5).

What did this mean? I wondered.

In Jeremiah's case these words of God had set in motion a chain of events in which the young prophet was mightly used to speak to his own people. The young prophet was to warn his people of the consequences of straying from Jehovah. He was to warn them, and at the same time, he was to assure them of God's undying love for them.

Was this to be my commission from my Father?

I read the words again. "I ordained thee a prophet unto the nations." How could these words be directed to me? I was but a young, quite unexperienced evangelist. I seemed impressed to keep on reading. As I did, verses 7 and 8 of the same chapter popped up at me. I read them aloud. Slowly.

"Say not, I am a child: for thou shalt go to all that I shall send thee, and whatsoever I command thee thou shalt speak. Be not afraid . . . I am with thee . . . I have put My Word in thy mouth."

"*Say not, I am a child . . .*"

So my youth was not to be considered a deterrent to the proclamation of God's Word.

". . . *thou shalt go to all that I shall send thee.*"

The commission was not to be of my own choosing.

"*I have put My Word in thy mouth.*"

He would even tell me what I was to say!

I don't remember how long I remained in His presence that day, praising Him as I considered this ordination or commission. But I do remember that the warm glow that accompanied God's Words to me remained for hours, and that the experience left a profound impression upon me.

"*Ordained unto the nations . . .*"

Sleep was a long time in coming to me that night.

As the days passed, I found myself thinking more and more about that special time with the Lord when He had spoken so clearly to me of that commission.

I searched the Scriptures to find further confirmation, and to my amazement, I learned that God never sought for a ministry, per se, to get a job done; He looked for a man. Then, when He had found the man, He gave him a ministry to perform. In other words, my ordination unto the nations had not been God's means of instituting a ministry. It had been His search for a man.

He had done the same with Jeremiah. And Isaiah. And all the others He called or "ordained unto the nations," as He had done me. And each in turn had responded, "Here am I, Lord. Send me." When God spoke to me so clearly that day, my response had been the same as theirs: "Here am I, Lord. Send me. And I will go."

The more I thought about the subject, the more I realized that I had often been guilty of postponing opportunities of serving the Lord by mentally delegating that particular task or responsibility to "a ministry." I should have known better. Because, each time that happened, God had simply been showing me— as he does everyone—that the so-called "major ministries" are not the sole proprietors of evangelism. Instead, evangelism is the major business of every believer.

After all, hadn't God told the Prophet Ezekiel, "I sought for *a man* (not a *ministry*, but a man) . . . that should make up the hedge, and stand in the gap before Me"? (Ezekiel 22:30). The more I pondered the significance of God's call to me, the more I realized both the importance and the universality of God's call.

I was both humbled and excited as I continued to respond, "Here am I Lord . . ."

COMPASSION: GOD'S KEY TO EVANGELISM

As the scores of little children crowded around Heidi and me, reaching out to touch us, I was reminded of how they had done the same with Jesus. But when they almost smothered us by their sheer numbers, I was tempted to push them aside. Then I remembered what Jesus said, "Let the children come unto Me . . . for of such is the Kingdom of Heaven . . ."

Heidi and I were spending some time in the civil-strife-torn country of Zimbabwe, and had been invited to speak to the military personnel by the Chaplain General of the Zimbabwean Armed Forces. This was our first time in Zimbabwe and we were appalled at the devastation we saw all about us, the inevitable result of war.

Even though Zimbabwe had gained its independence, it had paid a terribly high price for freedom. And now, with black leadership in control of the government, thousands of white Zimbabweans were fleeing the country, leaving hundreds of top-ranking positions and offices vacant. The result was chaos, with hardly anybody knowing from day to day who was in charge or what would happen.

The Chaplain General, an outspoken man of God with a burden for his entire nation—especially the military—had asked us to speak to the soldiers in the barracks. So our assignment was to go from one barracks to the other, opening the Word of God with the service personnel and their families.

"What will you be the subject of your message to the military, Keith?" the General asked me.

Before answering him, my mind flashed to the subject I had been focusing on for weeks: the compassion of Jesus, which I now realized was the centrality, the quintessence of God's love. And for days it seemed that I could hardly think of anything besides that wondrous love.

In answer to the General's question, I said, "Sir, I'm glad you asked. For weeks the Lord has been revealing to me the awesomeness and extent of His great love . . . the love that was demonstrated by the compassion of Jesus . . .

"So, General," I continued, "in response to the leading of the Holy Spirit, I'll be sharing the love of God: the powerful, revolutionary love of God. The love that's demonstrated by the compassion of Jesus."

He smiled slightly. "Revolutionary love? Since the men know all about revolution, that's very fitting."

The General sighed, and for the first time I was aware of the lines of fatigue around his eyes and mouth. Then he squared his shoulders and smiled. "But, Keith, our people must not only hear of the love of God. That love, depicted as you've just said, by the compassion of Jesus, must be demonstrated to them."

"Yes," I agreed, "if God's love is to be effective, it must be demonstrated. It must be demonstrated by every person, every soldier in the Lord's army. And if . . . I mean when that happens, because I believe that it one day will happen . . . the result would be such a demonstration of Jesus' compassion that it would shake nations."

The General smiled. "That's right, Keith. God bless you. Bless you as you minister in the barracks . . . and may God bless you and Heidi as you minister in Africa . . ."

His blessing became a benediction.

Throughout that day, I spoke in two different barracks of the revolutionary compassion of Jesus. "It's the compassionate love the world is waiting for," I said, "the love the world is literally dying for . . ."

And having so recently come from the battlefield, these men and women could identify with my words. Their response was overwhelming. Scores of service personnel responded to the love of God—as illustrated by the compassion of Jesus.

My thinking about Jesus' ministry became crystalized in a new way. I had often wondered why Jesus' ministry was so effective. Now I knew. Jesus' ministry was so powerful because it was motivated by love. In other words, the love, or *compassion* of God—that was exemplified by Jesus—was the motivating force behind Jesus' effectiveness.

As I preached and taught that day, I observed the hearers' response. In the truest sense of the world, they were not responding to me. They were responding to the living, dynamic love of God. And I realized that the love of God, or *compassion of God*—I believe the two terms are practically synonymous—are neither a "feeling" nor a human emotion. It was something much greater than that.

Then it came to me: Compassion is a force.

It's a very real, tangible motivating force. And as such, that force is the true key to evangelism!

I realized that when we demonstrate compassion, we are revealing God's love. And because God *is* love, when we share that love with others, then we are in a very real sense exposing them to God Himself! In other words, when the inexpressible love of God fills and floods a person and overflows into the life of another, that is the basis, the core of evangelism!

That realization excited me. And I began to imagine what would take place among the world's love-hungry, love-deprived masses if that latent, tremendous force of compassion—Jesus' compassion—were to be demonstrated by God's people. The concept fired my imagination. And I began to think of all the possibilities I had at my own disposal for demonstrating compassion to the poor, to the hungry, to the sick in body, the bound by sin, to all of the world's misdirected and *un*-directed people.

All the pieces of the "evangelism puzzle" began to fall into place. I reviewed the ministry of Jesus. Because He was motivated by His Father, He did only the things that pleased the Father. It follows, then, that Jesus was directed and motivated by the Father's compassion. And since God is the Author of Life itself, God's resources flowed in and through Him to those He ministered to. The inevitable result: Jesus' miracle ministry.

I realized I was onto something of tremendous significance. Jesus was God's love, His compassion in action. The fullness of the Father dwelt in Him. Therefore the infinite power of God operated through Him. When He pleased the Father, spoke God's

Words, demonstrated God's love, lives were changed and sick bodies were healed.

What happened? Supernatural results. In a word: miracles.

How did those miracles happen? Jesus simply received and acted upon the living Word of the Living God. And He did so in the same way that any child of God could do it. By faith.

When Jesus was confronted by those with leprosy desiring to be healed, Jesus was "moved with compassion" and the lepers were healed. (Mark 1:40-42) The formula was: Jesus' compassion, plus the recipients' faith.

When the two blind men cried out for mercy, Jesus "had compassion upon them," and they were healed: in response to His love and their faith.

It was through Jesus' miracle ministry of compassion that thousands came to Him for healing. They heard of His compassion, His love, His miracles, and they came to Him. And they received all that they came to find.

After completing our ministry in Zimbabwe, Heidi and I participated in a two-week crusade in the neighboring country of Zambia. Under the banner of "Consider Jesus and Live," we spent a week each on two different campuses to minister to both students and faculty. And it was while we ministered to students that we were confronted with a most unusual situation.

During those two weeks, Heidi and I scheduled our afternoons counseling college personnel, usually in different campus locations. One of those afternoons I was fellowshipping with some of the professors, and answering questions regarding their personal walk with the Lord. At the same time Heidi was witnessing and praying with several girls in their dormitory.

Suddenly I was surprised when one of those young ladies burst into the building just as my meeting was concluding. The girl's face was in an expression of near panic. I paused in mid-word, and all of us turned to face her.

"Keith . . . Keith . . . you've got to come . . .!" She leaned, panting, holding the door.

"Why? Where? What's the problem?"

"Heidi needs you . . ."

That was all I needed to hear. My wife was in trouble.

"Take me to her." Barely giving the girl time to catch her breath, I said, "What's the problem. Is something wrong with Heidi?"

She shook her head. "It's not Heidi . . . it's one of the girls we've been praying for . . ."

"What do you mean?"

"Heidi had been sharing with all of us . . . then she said, 'Now we're going to pray.' It was when we started to pray that it happened. That's when she did it . . ."

"When who did what?" I asked impatiently.

"It was one of the girls. She began acting crazy. She went into a rage. It was like something took control of her . . ."

"Has she ever done this before?"

The girl nodded. "Yes."

"And what have you done when it happens?" I asked.

"We didn't know what to do. Nothing seems to work. Sometimes she carries on like that for hours . . . and then she'll be okay. We don't understand . . ."

At that moment, Heidi met us. She looked upset. "What's happening?" I asked.

"A girl is possessed with a devil," she said. "I've been commanding the evil spirit to come out . . . the other girls are praying . . . nothing seems to be happening . . . so I sent for you."

I could hear the tormented girl's screams long before we got to the room. I had to push my way through the crowd of curious bystanders who were lining the hallway and trying to peer into the room. When they saw me, they moved aside to let the three of us into the room. It was jammed with students.

As I made my way to the girl's side, I noted that there were a few new converts there as well. "Good," I thought, "This will be a good demonstration to them of God's compassion."

The tormented girl was stretched out full length on the floor in the center of the room. She was thrashing around in total abandon, her face and body contorting and twisting as though she was in the grip of some terrible pain or being. Her eyes were fixed and glassy, staring at nothing or anybody in particular. The girl's mouth was opened wide and she was screaming at the top of her lungs.

I moved to the girl's side and looked down upon her in compassion. She was clearly out of her own control, as much out of control as the man amongst the tombs had been. And I remembered that when Jesus healed that desperate man, He had reminded the now-healed, sane man that he had arrived at this condition because, "the Lord hath . . . had *compassion* on thee" (Mark 5:19). In that brief moment when I stood looking down upon the pitiful sight before me, my heart was filled with compassion. I knew I was in for a battle, perhaps the battle of my life. I knew in my heart that I would not be dealing with a mere human adversary of ordinary flesh and blood. I realized I was about to engage in hand-to-hand conflict with the Enemy of men's souls: with the principalities and powers the Apostle Paul described in Ephesians 6:12.

"Let's pick her up and put her on the bed," I said.

As we tried to move her, she increased her frantic activity to such a degree that it required six strong men to get hold of her and move her to the bed. And once upon the bed, it took five to keep her there.

Oblivious to the stares of the curious onlookers, I moved to the side of the stricken girl and addressed the demon who was in control of her. With a loud voice I said, "In Jesus Name, you foul spirit, come out! Come out in Jesus' Name! Come out!"

Nothing happened, except that the girl's rage intensified.

I prayed again. "I take authority over you, in Jesus' Name. You have no right to afflict this girl. You have no right to be here in this place. I rebuke you in Jesus' Name. And I command you to come out and depart from her!"

Nothing happened.

I prayed with even greater fervor, with seemingly no effect whatsoever. When none of the usual exorcising resulted in freeing the girl from the demon's grip, I realized this was not a "usual" attack. I was obviously dealing with one of Satan's strongholds.

It was then that I remembered the advice given me by some of my African evangelist friends. "Casting out demons is serious business," one man told me. "And you You should always make eye contact with the possessed person. Command the evil spirit to look at you, and to identify himself . . ."

With the girl's head jerking and thrusting from side to side, I saw that eye contact with her would be difficult if not impossible. So I gripped her head with my hands. Still she would not look at me. Even when I held my face close to hers, the girl evaded my eye contact by rolling her eyes from side to side.

I gripped the girl's head in both my hands and tried to focus upon her rapidly moving eyes. "Identify yourself, you evil spirit!" I commanded. "Who are you? Tell me your name!"

The only response was a chorus of even more ghastly screams.

I refused to give up, refused to be defeated. "Come out in Jesus' Name. You have no power over this girl or in this place. You must come out in Jesus' Name!"

The girl's contortions increased, but suddenly the demon began speaking back to me.

"No! No! No! No! No!" it cried out in a harsh voice, totally unlike the girl's own voice. "No! No! No!" Then it laughed, a horrible, spine-chilling, high-pitched voice. "No! No! No!" it shouted over and over again as the girl's body was shaken and bent.

Progress was being made. I knew it. I did not let up. "You foul spirit, you must come out of her, in Jesus' Name. You are coming out of her . . . right now!" I shouted at the demon who was trying to destroy this girl.

For ten minutes I prayed and commanded. Fifteen minutes. Twenty minutes went by as I prayed, interceded, and commanded the demon to depart. My voice became tired and my body ached as though I was actually being pummelled by a physical foe. Within minutes I was sweating profusely and my clothes were soaked.

From others I learned that this girl had desired to

experience God's love and power in her life. But something prevented this from happening? All that I knew at the moment was that her body and mind were being dominated by forces she could not control.

I continued to pray. I continued to command the demon to depart. "Come out, in Jesus' Name!" I shouted.

Suddenly God reminded me of a meeting in which the pastor had led the congregation in a time of laughing at the devil. So I said, "I laugh at you, you foul spirit, because you are a defeated foe. Jesus stripped you of all your authority and power. Ha, ha, ha! I laugh at you. Ha, ha, ha! You are defeated. So come out . . . come out!"

The demon tore the girl mightly. Then departed, leaving the girl limp and weak. She relaxed upon the bed and opened her eyes. When she saw the room full of people, she sat up suddenly, her eyes wide. "Why are they all here?"

"Don't you know?" I asked.

"No . . . no, I don't," she said.

It was then that I realized that the girl had actually been totally out of control, and had had no idea of what was going on. When I told her, she asked, "Is it because I went to the witch doctor . . .?"

"Witch doctor? When did you go to a witch doctor?"

Her lips trembled. "One week ago . . . it was before you came to my country. I had been sick . . . and he . . . he helped me. I took some medicine that he gave me and . . ."

"The witch doctor gave you some medicine?" I asked.

"Yes. I have it there in my bag."

"Let me have it," I said, then explained to her how she had opened herself up to demon possession by allowing the witch doctor to administer his evil incantations and rites to her. She handed me a newspaper-wrapped package. I opened it and found an evil-looking substance inside.

"Now, if you will renounce all works of darkness . . . and confess Jesus the Lord of your life . . . you will become free," I told her. "Is this what you want to do?"

"Yes . . . yes, that is what I want," she responded eagerly.

"Then, let's pray," I said. "You tell the Lord what you have just told me, and we will complete the transaction right now."

With no comment I took the medicine and flushed it down the toilet.

The flush of victory and peace was upon her face when we left her in the college dormitory that day. Later, one of the girl's close friends told Heidi, "My girlfriend is really free. Really free! There has been a great change in her life. Praise the Lord, He really does set us free!"

I praised God for the girl's release and victory. But I also praised God that I was learning how to minister with His very own "compassion power"!

9

HE THAT GOETH FORTH WEEPING . . .

Compassion power. I was seeing how compassion power worked. But how did one receive it? How did one learn to minister in it? Now that I had become aware of the impact of such power, I was determined that I would continually seek to move and operate in this remarkable power.

Actually, the move in that direction began even before I left South Africa. Just a few nights before leaving South Africa, to minister in Zimbabwe and Zambia, Heidi and I were attending our "home church" in Petermeritzburg. Just prior to the service the pastor indicated he'd like to talk to me, so I walked over to where he was.

"Keith, would you like to speak tonight . . . and share what's on your heart . . . and where the Lord is leading you when you leave here?" he asked.

"Of course. I'd be very glad to do so," I said.

"Good. I'll call for you to come up here in a few minutes. I want you to take your time. Feel very free to share with us for as long as the Lord leads you to do so."

I thanked him and started back for my seat. On the outside I may have looked calm. But on the inside I was far from calm. I was bursting with excitement. Heidi and I had attended this church for as long as we'd been in South Africa. We loved it and considered it our home church. Though I had ministered to various groups in the congregation, and on occasion represented the church by preaching in open air evangelistic services, I had never ministered to this body as a whole. I had long desired to do so. Now my opportunity had come, and I was elated.

During those moments before the pastor called me up, I sat quietly in prayer, asking the Lord to show me what I was to say. Almost before I realized it, I heard the pastor inviting me to the front. He gave me an introduction, and then . . . he sat down and Heidi and I were standing alone on the platform—facing the congregation of people.

I began . . .

"It's a great joy for me to be able to share with you of God's goodness to us . . . before Heidi and I leave your country and begin preaching the Gospel of the Kingdom in other parts of Africa . . ."

I thanked the people for their warmth, for the fellowship we had enjoyed. I thanked them for their unfailing support.

"God has been faithful to us . . ." I went on. "But He is always faithful to us when we have been faithful to His Word. Because He always confirms His Word with wonders."

A powerful "Amen!" response thundered through the building.

"We all know that people of every race and every

nation are longing to know Him, and to know the power of His resurrection. I know this and you know this . . ."

The people were giving me their undivided attention. I could see and hear and actually *feel* their response.

"By the grace of God," I continued, "Heidi and I have seen hundreds of people come to Christ. We have had the privilege of working with Muslims . . . and Buddhists . . . and Hindus . . . and leading them to Jesus . . ."

As I spoke those last words, something happened. I stopped speaking and began to weep. I tried to speak, but no words would come. All I could do was weep. Uncontrollably. "What is happening to me?" I wondered.

I simply could not speak. I could not form words. I turned to Heidi, who was standing next to me. She was looking at me but said nothing. I continued to weep . . .

A strange phenomenon took place. As I wept, others in the congregation began to weep. Finally after a seeming eternity, one man shouted, "Let's give Jesus a praise offering!"

The response was instantaneous. The applause was thunderous. It seemed to shake the very rafters of the building. It reverberated from wall to wall. And still the people applauded. Shouts of praise and hallelujahs rang throughout the building. And still I wept. And others wept as I did.

The pastor came to the microphone. "If he can't speak, I guess he's no good," he jokingly said to Heidi. "Do you have something to say?"

I stepped back and Heidi spoke a few words of exhortation and handed the microphone back to the pastor. Still I could not speak, but continued to weep. We returned to our seats. The Spirit of God came upon me that night as never before in my life. As I wept it seemed that a cleansing took place . . .

Still I wept. At first I had been embarrassed, then I knew this was a sovereign work of the Lord. It seemed that I was enveloped by the Holy Spirit. The old Keith was consumed by His love and a new and different, a more compassionate Keith was emerging. I was aware of that compassion. Compassion for the weak, the sinful, the sick, the helpless . . .

When Jesus saw the multitudes, He was moved with compassion. And it was that compassion that motivated Him to minister to the thousands who be-sieged Him day and night. It was that compassion that caused Him to send out the 70 with orders to "Heal the sick, cleanse the lepers, raise the dead, cast out devils . . ."

It was because of that compassion that Jesus initi-ated His Great Commission, urging His followers to "Go . . . into all the world . . ." with His heart-changing, life-renewing message of hope, and love, and redemption, and peace.

The end result of Jesus' compassionate love, was the actual *delegation* of His very own power to those who became one with Him! He gave them power of attorney to speak in His Name, to act in His stead, to live His very own life of power in the earth.

That night, it came to me with dynamic force: it was compassion that motivated Jesus. It was His compassion that was the motivating force behind His ministry. During that service, I was caught up in Je-sus' compassion: for all people, for all nations. And I knew that compassion was biw to be my main motivation in ministry. Hereafter, I would minister as He had done.

Which meant that compassion, Jesus' compassion, would be the motivating force behind everything I did! As it was with Jesus, His very own compassionate love *grafted into me* would then prepare the way for His miracle ministry wherever I went.

As I wept in silence before the Lord that night, that weeping seemed to spread throughout the congregation.

At the conclusion of the service, two men from different parts of the sanctuary came to me, both of them weeping. One of them said, "I have been unable to cry for many years . . . but tonight as you were speaking, and then began to weep, I began to weep . . . as I had never done before."

I laid my hand upon his shoulder. "Brother," I told him, "if you allow the compassion of God, and the burden for others, to rise up within you, weeping will never again be a problem."

It was during those two weeks in the beautiful country of Zambia, in central Africa, that I began to experience the power of Jesus' compassion in my own ministry. And once I began to minister as Jesus did, I realized I would never be satisfied with anything less.

At the close of the Zambia campaign, though we had shared the love of God with hundreds, we had barely scratched the surface of the country's five and one-half million people. And as we were preparing to leave to minister in Kenya, Heidi and I were reminiscing.

Jesus, in His High Priestly prayer to the Father, defined both our calling and our commission. "As Thou hast sent Me into the world," he prayed, "even so have I *also sent them into the world . . .*"

"That was Jesus' desire and plan," I told Heidi, "and now that's exactly what we are doing—He has sent us into the world, and we are now going into the world . . ."

"All across Africa," Heidi said.

"Yes, that's a good beginning."

And Jesus' purpose in all of this, I recalled, was unity. Unity of Kingdom people. Jesus' prayer made that clear: "That they all may be one; as Thou, Father, art in Me, and I in Thee, that they also may be one in Us: *that the world may believe* that Thou hast sent Me."

During our time in Africa, we had witnessed and been a part of that unity, which had resulted in a rich harvest. I recalled the tremendous revival we'd been a part of in Blantyre, Malawi, where over 8,000 made commitments to Christ. And, of course, our Gospel witness in the countries of Zambia and Zimbabwe and South Africa was still fresh in my mind.

Before leaving Malawi our team prayed together and praised God for His visitation among us during those excitement packed days and nights. I was humbled by and will never forget the words of an older Anglican priest who had ministered with us.

"These two weeks have changed my life," he said. "Prior to this time I had never seen God do what He did during these short weeks. It was exciting, even startling, to see people come to the Lord as we've seen them do . . ."

"It's been wonderful," I agreed. "Really wonderful."

He nodded. "And I can readily see that it came about because we all came together—in unity and agreement—and expected to see God's blessing. Then He worked the miracles . . ."

He was silent for a few moments, but I could see that he had something more to say.

Soon he sighed. "My only regret is that I didn't learn this secret earlier in my ministry . . . instead of during the closing years of my life."

The he smiled. "Nevertheless, everything I have learned has truly changed my life and ministry. And I have been renewed to go forth in the power of the Holy Spirit . . ."

There it was again: unity. Unity commingled with compassion. That mixture had drawn many denominational church leaders into a common bond of oneness in the Body of Christ. The so-called "mainline" evangelical and Pentecostal churches had joined forces with a number of independent churches and a wide spectrum of Christian organizations. The result had been revival.

As we had come together during those weeks, we came together for a single purpose—which we had accomplished. We hadn't come to discuss our theological differences or our worship preferences. We had come together to lift up Jesus in compassionate unity. And when we did that, the Holy Spirit controlled us all.

I was struck by the power of unity.

Jesus had prayed for that unity.

And on the Day of Pentecost the believers had demonstrated unity. The result had been the powerful outpouring of God's Spirit in one time and place such as had never been seen before. That unity had released power, the power to add a record 3,000 souls to the Lord *in one day*!

Unity of believers.

I was learning the importance of that unity. And I was seeing that when believers join their faith with one another (that's unity), the life of God will be powerfully manifested.

That unity of the brethren was illustrated in the Gospel account and a palsied man desired healing. Since the house was jammed with people, there was no way that a man on a stretcher could be brought in. So four friends combined their efforts (that's unity), ripped a hole in the roof, and lowered the man into the house directly in front of the Master.

Jesus saw their faith: the result of their unity. He saw the corporate faith of the five men, one patient and four friends. And the unity Jesus saw released healing into the palsied man's body. He was immediately healed and restored.

Only unity in faith can enable believers to bring down the strongholds of Satan. Only through unity in faith can two believers put ten thousand to flight (whereas one can chase one thousand). Unity in faith greatly magnifies the power that's available to one believer!

As Heidi and I returned to East Africa, Psalm 126:6 was more firmly embedded in our hearts than ever before, "He that goeth forth and weepeth, bearing precious seed shall doubtless come again with rejoicing, bringing his sheaves with him."

10

PERFECTED FRUIT

Cool dawn was breaking as we approached the border between Kenya and Uganda, and the red-orbed tropical sun was just slipping from behind the rugged hills of Kenya. Heidi and I had just spent a few days in Nairobi finalizing details for the upcoming Middle East Christian Leadership Conference, and we were on our way to spend a week with John and Mary Wilson in Uganda.

A native of Uganda, John Wilson was an outstanding evangelist and had spearheaded the ministry of reconciliation between Arab and Christian leaders in the Middle East. Since we were involved to some degree in the Middle East, John invited us to go with him to Uganda and lay plans for the Conference as well as consider further reconciliation ministries in Uganda.

John and other nationals had told us much about the horror-filled years under the despotical hands of Idi Amin, and how he had turned the beautiful, garden-like Uganda into a blood-bathed shambles.

During his iron-fisted reign, Amin had instigated the torture of and murder of more than half a million Ugandans, one of them the outstanding spiritual leader of the Anglican Church, Archbishop Juwani Lawum.

"Did you know the Archbishop?" I asked John Wilson as we stood in line at the border to have our visas approved and our passports cleared.

He nodded. "Yes, very well. Juwani Lawum was a friend. We miss him very much."

As we inched our way forward in the line, I could not but think of Uganda, and of the endless nightmare the Ugandan people had endured under Amin's cruel dictatorship.

With our approved and stamped passports in our hands, John Wilson took the wheel of our Volkswagen van and we were soon dodging the deep chuck holes that pitted the Ugandan highway system. Despite John's frequent swerving of the van to miss those holes, Heidi and I enjoyed the scenery: the lush, fertile farmland of the nation that had once rightly been called the "Pearl of Africa." Before Amin's reign Uganda had been a progressive, efficiently run agricultural nation, the breadbasket for much of Africa, a fact that was no longer true. John told us that due to the destruction Idi Amin had wreaked upon every part and parcel of this land, Uganda's once prosperous economy has tragically ground nearly to a standstill.

I was thinking about Idi Amin and wondering about the man's seeming obsessive desire to destroy this land, when I was jarred from my revery by John's words. "There's the first one . . ."

"The first what?" Heidi asked.

"Our first roadblock of the day."

I looked up in time to see a handful of armed soldiers lined up across the road in front of us. One of them was motioning for us to stop. John slowed and pulled the Volkswagen over to the side of the highway.

A youthful Ugandan soldier swaggered over and peered into our vehicle. When he saw John Wilson's Episcopal priest's collar, his manner changed. And when he spoke, he did so with respect. The two conversed in an Ugandan dialect for a couple of minutes, then John handed him some Gospel literature and the man waved us on.

"This is just the beginning," John told us as we were once again rolling. "We'll have these roadblocks every few miles . . . sometimes even closer together than that."

"What's the purpose of them?" I asked.

He shrugged. "Mostly graft," he said. "He allowed us to pass because I'm a minister. But they extract a bribe from most people before they allow them to continue on their way."

"Is it legal?"

He shrugged again. "Not really. It's just one of the lawless remnants of Idi Amin's administration that we'll have to put up with until the country gets on its feet again."

True to John's words, we did meet up with other roadblocks, some of them within a few hundred yards of each other. They slowed us down considerably, but we finally arrived at the outskirts of the once beautiful capital city of Kampala.

We drove in silence through the mostly empty streets of this formerly modern, bustling city. The evidence of Amin's savage destruction was everywhere. The city was a shambles, a mere shadow of it's earlier glory. Streets and sidewalks were littered with trash and garbage and the stench from heaps of decaying garbage filled the air.

The few people we saw on the streets were moving about aimlessly, their faces fixed with expressions of despair and hopelessness. Little more needed to be said. Idi Amin had murdered more than people. He had also killed the hope of most of those who had survived his butchery.

At the church guest house Roberta met us and showed us to the room where we would stay while in Kampala. We soon learned first hand of the further extent of the city's decadent condition. Even the church guest house boasted of no running water or toilet facilities. And the electrical service was sporadic. It was clearly evident that Uganda, at least in the capital city, was bereft of the basic necessities to maintain even the bare minimum of health and hygiene.

As she was trying to make us comfortable, we asked Roberta of her experiences under Idi Amin. An expression of pain slid across the young woman's face. "My husband . . ." she began, "they took him from me . . . and murdered him . . ."

"How awful," Heidi gasped.

Roberta nodded. "But that wasn't all they did. They took my family . . . most of them . . . and killed them too." Heidi and I listened with growing horror as Roberta gave us a brief description of her own personal suffering.

"How could you keep on living after all that?" I asked.

Roberta smiled bravely and as she did, the lines of suffering were temporarily erased. "God's love," she said simply. "It was His love that made the difference.

118

During the persecutions the Christians joined together for prayer and fellowship . . . and we found His love to be steadfast and strong."

While Roberta spoke of the personal suffering and tragedy that had impacted her life, my eyes were drawn to her face. The woman bore a look of undisturbed peace, an evident reflection of the supernatural joy that God's love had implanted within her.

Before we tried to rest, Heidi and I discussed and tried to grasp the enormity of the suffering endured by the Ugandans. But we could not identify with Roberta or with the many others from whom we heard similar stories of horror. We had never experienced anything that prepared us for this.

That afternoon we caught a glimpse of the unity Roberta had tried to describe, the unity that had preserved their spirits and kept them alive. We were invited to attend what they termed their "revival meeting," which was a time when the believers met to encourage one another in the faith by sharing testimonies of God's goodness and His miraculous intervention in their lives.

The meeting was held at the Anglican Church Hall. By the time we arrived, we found it already quite full of expectantly waiting people. Despite the evident marks of suffering each of them bore, they praised God with gusto and shared vibrant testimonies of His goodness to them.

I was asked to extend Christian greetings to my Ugandan brothers and sisters and to share the Word with them. When I had finished and sat down, I looked at the faces around me. Though they had all suffered, most of them radiated the joy of the Lord.

I thought of that joy. As with all believers, their joy had sprung from a seed once planted, grown to maturity—to perfection—then harvested. It came from the life of God received into the fertile soil of eager hearts, where it had been nurtured and brought to fruition. That's what Jesus had been talking about when He spoke of bearing fruit.

"I am the vine," Jesus told His disciples that day, "you are the branches. He who abides in Me, and I in him, bears *much fruit* (emphasis the author's). . . . By this My Father is glorified, that you bear much fruit. . . . I chose you and appointed you that you should go and bear fruit, and that your fruit should remain" (John 15:5, 8, 16).

Fruit that *remains*, I realized, is fruit that has come to maturity or perfection. It is fruit that "bears" yet other fruit, fruit that quite literally reproduces itself by spawning additional fruit of like nature.

These Ugandans I was hearing were that kind of fruit.

No wonder Uganda and other East African nations were experiencing revival: they had become perfected fruit and were simply doing what they had come into existence to do—bear fruit.

Suddenly I realized I had the answer to a question I had been asking for a number of months. How could converts be transfused into the mainstream of the Kingdom? We had seen thousands come to God during our African campaigns, but without followup, we knew that many of these converts would never attain majority, and that they would atrophy, die on the vine.

How could this attrition rate be slowed or stopped?

I was seeing the answer before me: perfected fruit.

Revival, genuine, God-sent revival, would result in many conversions. And if those new babes in Christ, that embryonic fruit, was to become mature, it must of necessity be surrounded by strong, mature models. In other words: perfected fruit, or those in whom the life of God had grown to maturity. Those models would be the ones who had walked with Jesus, who had weathered the storms and stood the tests.

If such men and women would demonstrate their living fruit to the new converts—which is the essence of discipling and discipleship—the leakage would be stopped, these immature ones would grow in the grace and knowledge of God and Jesus' desire would be accomplished, i.e., the "fruit would remain."

Such commitment to each other, I knew, would be expensive. But it would be worth the cost!

These thoughts brought to mind Stephen Lungu, an African evangelist and dear friend and brother in Christ. While ministering together recently in Malawi, Stephen had shared stories that illustrated the effects of personal commitment, commitment that had resulted in perfected fruit.

One day as we were walking down the street in Blantyre, Stephen pointed to a man across the street. "That man's name is James," Stephen said. "James is one of my spiritual children. Let me tell you how James came to the Lord . . ."

My friend then related story after story of how numerous men and women had come to the Lord through his ministry. I was amazed. I had met a number of those godly people, and all of them seemed to be examples of "perfected fruit." How did that happen? I wondered.

"During the middle 60's," Stephen continued, "the Spirit of God led me to minister in a very difficult area, up in the brush area of northern Malawi . . ."

He paused as though remembering. "I ministered for three months in that malaria-infested region," he said. "And it was a hard, thankless time. There were none who were receptive to the message I preached. I became discouraged. I wanted to quit. Yet I held on. And now I'm glad I did."

"What happened?" I asked.

"Well, during that entire three months of ministry, there was one—only one—person who accepted my message, and who turned to Jesus . . ."

"In three months?" I was aghast.

"That's right. Only one in three months."

A shadow of a smile came to my friend's lips. He turned to the man who was with us. "Keith, I want you to meet him . . . that man who came to Jesus during that time . . ."

The man Stephen referred to grinned broadly as he thrust out his hand and gripped mine. "This is the man?" I asked in amazement. "Are you telling me that Major Jimu is that convert?"

Stephen nodded. "Yes. he is that man."

I had become well acquainted with Major Jimu sometime earlier as a man of God, one who exemplified the perfected fruit we had been discussing. In fact, I thought, all of the converts I knew who had come to the Lord through Stephen's ministry seemed to be the kind of fruit that Jesus spoke of, fruit that "remained": perfected fruit. How did this happen so consistently?

I looked around me at this gathering in the Anglican Church Hall. And I "saw" them for the first time as those who had not always been this stable. Their fruit had not always been as mature and completed.

And now I knew how these suffering ones had come through with their spiritual lives intact. I knew how they had survived.

They had been discipled.

Mature believers had discipled them until they could stand alone. That's what Stephen had done in Malawi. He had discipled his converts. He had walked with them through the fires of their personal oppression. He had led them in the paths of righteousness. One by one, he had taught them the way, he had shown them how to live for God.

And he had stayed with them until each of them had grown strong and stable, with the ability to perfect the fruit in others. Then each of those "perfected fruit" converts had gone out, planted seed and repeated the cycle.

I knew now what had taken place in Uganda. The perfected ones had discipled their converts until they were mature. And in the doing of it they had promulgated revival fires that had outlasted the fires of persecution and hell foisted upon them by a mad dictator.

That was the way to go. Jesus said, "Go and make disciples. Then teach (or disciple) those disciples. Teach them until they are ready to make a long-lasting commitment to Me and My Word. Then baptize them, and teach (disciple) them some more" (author's paraphrase of Matthew 28:19,20).

Sitting there in that Anglican Church Hall that day, in the midst of ruined Uganda, I realized that my task, my commission, was to obey Jesus' command.

And I determined to do my part!

11

DEAR LORD, DON'T LET US FAIL

"We can't bring up or discuss any sensitive, potentially explosive issues," I patiently explained to each of the Jewish delegates one at a time. "We must remember that our purpose is spiritual, not political . . ."

Nodding in the affirmative, Joel spoke. "I agree. My only desire is share the love of God with my Jewish and Arab brothers and sisters. And I know that this can only be accomplished if all of us agree to bring up nothing about our respective countries, or the State of Israel."

Our hearts were gladdened and relieved when we realized that Joel had voiced the concensus of the group.

Heidi and I were in Israel, wrapping up the final details of the upcoming long-awaited, five-day Middle East meeting designed to reconcile spiritual leaders. As the target date for this conference approached, the pace had quickened and the pressures had mounted.

This had been evident as we had left Nairobi, Kenya, bound for Tel Aviv.

Before boarding that flight for Israel, Heidi and I had undergone an intensive search of our luggage. Apparently the Israeli officials were suspicious of our travel motives since we had been out of the United States for nearly a year. In all our dealings with Customs and Security, we had never seen our luggage taken apart piece by piece as we saw in Nairobi.

I prayed they would not find the extensive list of Arab and Jewish believers I had amassed. Finally the search was over. The inspector smiled and stamped our passports. With a final nod, he waved us through Security and onto the airplane. I checked my watch. The search had taken a full hour.

Nairobi behind us, we rested, mentally preparing ourselves for our short, but very important stop in Israel to brief the Israeli delegates and to make the final transportation arrangements. The complex details were eventually finalized and Heidi and I flew to Athens where we boarded the "Flying Dolphin," the hydrofoil that would take us to our rendezvous.

Now Greece's shoreline receded behind us, as Heidi and I stood at the rail, marveling at our craft's speed as it smoothly skimmed the surface of the gloriously blue Mediteranean. We were alone, since we had arranged to arrive a few days prior to the convention to complete the hotel accommodations for our guests.

We had located the tiny island we were speeding toward quite by "accident." Several months ago we had been meeting in Athens with some of the conference delegates. It had been agreed that the meeting must be held in some secluded and neutral spot.

"It must also be private and quiet," John Wilson said when he spoke to me by phone from Nairobi.

"Both our Arab and Jewish friends will be sensitive to the location. The hotel must be large enough to accommodate all the delegates, but small enough so we will occupy the total facilities."

I voiced my agreement.

As I did, John continued. "Keith, how about you locating the facility? Make all the arrangements. Possibly on Crete, or Rhodes . . . or one of the other islands?"

I realized this was a critically important assignment. And since Heidi and I had only two more days remaining before we were scheduled to leave Greece to deal with other commitments. Aware of my hesitation, John pressed. "How about it, Keith. Do you think you can do it?"

I responded slowly. "I'll do my best."

"Good," John said, "then it's settled."

Aboard the Flying Dolphin, I took Heidi's hand. "Do you remember how we found this island?"

"How could I forget?" she responded.

With less than two days to look, I had tried to arrange a flight to the islands John had mentioned. The travel clerks shook their head. "Impossible," they said. "All the flights are full."

"Any possibility of a cancelation?" I asked.

"Not during tourist season," they assured me.

Finally I arranged for us to take a one-day cruise amongst the Greek islands, to visit as many hotels as possible.

"Do you remember that cruise?" I asked Heidi.

"It was beautiful . . . like it is today," she said.

"It was quite an adventure," I said, "and really a special answer to prayer that we found that little hotel."

I pointed. "I think that's our island directly

ahead . . ."

Moments later my observation was verified as our
captain skillfully maneuvered the Flying Dolphin
within a quarter mile of the little wharf and cut the
engines. The hydrofoil obediently slowed and sank to
the surface of the water. As we approached the dock
we could see the quaint little shops that lined the
main street of the tiny village.

A twenty-minute taxi ride brought us to the opposite side of the island where our hotel was located.
The driver had taken us through lovely rolling hills
covered with pistachio orchards, and a landscape that
was dotted here and there with small Greek Orthodox churches, which testified to the religious tradition
of the islanders.

Painted blue and white, the old, but well-kept hotel
complex was nestled picturesquely on the Mediterranean Sea Shore. It fit the necessary qualifications:
quiet, secluded, just the right size. Its sixty rooms
would adequately house the expected eighty-five delegates. And with the tourist season not yet begun, the
only people around would be the local residents.

"Heidi," I rejoiced, "it's just perfect for the conference."

She nodded and smiled in agreement.

Later I met with Malcolm Graham, who, with myself, were responsible for coordinating all the logistics
for this landmark gathering. Though we expected
eighty-five delegates from a dozen or so countries, we
had no assurance that even near that number would
arrive. And of course, registration was made even
more complex because of the difficulty and complex-
ity of getting any sort of telephone or written com-
munications either into or out of some of the Arab
countries.

Fortunately, both Malcolm and I had a sense of humor which helped us to handle our somewhat demanding responsibilities. "This whole thing's going to be like a circus . . ." he told me that night.

"Circus?" I asked. "What do you mean?"

"And a sensitive, three-ring circus at that," he said, "getting people off the airplane, into the boat and into the hotel. And then, when we get them into the hotel, to make each of them comfortable . . ." he paused for emphasis. ". . . and to make them happy with each other."

"No doubt about it," I said.

A trace of a smile played around his mouth. "So, I'll make a deal with you, Keith?" he said.

"A deal?" I said cautiously. "What kind of a deal?"

Straight-faced, he said, "I'll take the responsibility of making them happy at the hotel?"

"And . . .? What's my part in this deal?"

"I think you should have the exalted privilege of picking them up at the airport and getting them and their luggage transferred over here to the island."

I laughed. "Malcolm, they're both "exciting" projects. But, you've got a deal. I'll take you up on it."

We both had an inkling of how frustrating a job we'd be faced with. On the one hand, neither of us had any idea of when some of our people would arrived at the airport. I would just have to be on hand to meet every plane from certain countries, then arrange for taxis and boats to get them all to the island. But, on the other hand, we knew we had an explosive situation on our hands at the hotel. Mixing and intermingling Arabs and Jews would be very ticklish at best.

Nevertheless, we both agreed that Malcolm had probably gotten the better part of the deal. Heidi and

I thoroughly enjoyed and respected Malcolm as a friend and brother. Because, despite the pressures he faced during the days that followed he was inveterately cheerful and optimistic, a Christian gentleman. And on more than one occasion the three of us would use humor and laughter to weather a potentially explosive moment.

Two days before the arrival of our delegation, our plans and arrangements were complete, the three of us were taking tea in the hotel restaurant with a couple of early-arriving Palestinian brothers. One of these men listened quietly to our conversation for a while, then could contain himself no longer.

"Do all the delegates realize that there are going to be *Jewish* people here?" he asked, his voice shrill with panic.

Before I could answer him, he went on. "If they come without knowing Jews are going to be here, they'll walk out of the conference. They won't stay here."

"Why is that?" I asked, knowing the sensitivity of the situation, but wanting to hear from him.

"Because they'll consider it far too dangerous to meet with Jews for one thing . . . And, for another . . ." He paused without finishing the sentence.

"What's the other thing?" I asked.

"Because they'll be afraid that such knowledge would destroy their ministries in all of the Muslim countries."

I made eye contact with each one at the table before I spoke. "We've made every possible effort to avoid trouble," I said. "We have informed all of the leaders in each country with the full particulars of the situation, as well as a listing of all of the delegates, *and* the program agenda."

The Palestinians seemed not to be mollified.

"Furthermore," I went on, "we have appointed a man in each country to be the liaison between all of his country's delegates. And we've given him all the details of the consultation, with instructions to brief each of his country's delegates."

Still the Palestinians seemed uneasy. "It's too risky to have them meet with us," one of them said. "And such a meeting has potential for more harm than good for the Kingdom . . ."

He paused and took a deep breath. "For the good of all," he began, "you should call the Jewish delegation . . . and tell them to cancel their trip. Tell them not to come."

"Cancel their coming?" I asked. Then, rather cautiously I asked, "Why should the fear of fellowship with a brother in Christ—despite his nationality—hinder or disqualify any of us from participating in a joint meeting such as this?"

I looked around the circle. "If any of the delegates are fearful of being here—with either Jews or Arabs—they should eliminate themselves and choose not to come. But we should not eliminate our brothers from Israel on the basis of someone else's fears."

I knew I had said what needed to be said. We had worked too hard and too long with our brothers and sisters from these many nations for the plan to fail now. We had believed were were being led of the Lord. Now we must act upon that belief.

As the group concluded the discussion, the Spirit of God prevailed in our midst. I could sense, then see the tension easing. And the concensus of those present was to proceed as planned. There would be no last minute calls to revoke anyone's invitation. Under God the conference would materialize.

The conference began Monday afternoon at 4:00 P.M., but I missed the opening session. In fact, I missed the first evening entirely. I was meeting delegates at the Athens airport Monday afternoon and arranging their boat transportation to the island. But their planes were delayed for so long that by the time I met them and gathered my people together, the last boats for the island had already left, so we had to stay overnight in Athens.

Tuesday morning when I arrived with a load of delegates, I saw Heidi at the registration table where she had worked diligently for the past two days.

"How are things going?" I asked her.

"Quite well," she said cautiously. She looked around to see if we were alone, then lowered her. "But some of the people seem to be quite irritated and upset about something. And I don't know what's bothering them."

I nodded. "I thought so," I said, "the tension is so thick in here you could cut it with a knife."

I looked around. From where I stood I could see delegates from Jordan, Israel, Syria, Egypt, Iran, Cyprus, Turkey, Greece, Lebannon, Algeria, plus a few others from several Mediteranean and European countries.

"It's oppressive here," I said. "And it feels like the place is filled with fear . . ."

The first meetings I attended were disappointing. Delegates from each nation kept to themselves, steadfastly refusing to mix with others. This was noticeably so between the Jews and Arabs, who kept a set distance between each other, almost as though each believed the other group to be contaminated. And the fellowship, if it could even be called that, was shallow and superficial.

And as the day progressed, instead of an easing of the tensions, they noticeably increased. In discouragement and near desperation, I prayed, "Dear God, have we come this far only to fail?"

12

IN THE MIDST OF A MIRACLE

The uneasiness and tensions I sensed the second day were but a harbinger of what was to come. The first speaker on that eventful third day was to speak on the topic, "Crunch Questions for the Middle East Church." There was no way for us to know that his message would provide a "crunch" for the entire assembly.

The speaker was a British clergyman who had been working in Jerusalem during the past few years. He had hardly opened his mouth when I realized he was totally ignoring the principles we had laid down.

"This morning I want to address three particular questions," he began.

The first, "When and how are we going to take seriously the evangelism of the Muslim world in the Middle East?" Secondly, quoting Ezekiel concerning the Jewish people, "Can these dry bones live?" And finally, "What about the land of promise?"

As I heard the man list those questions, I had a premonition of what was to come. And I was right. Point by point the speaker proceded to meddle in all of the ills that were present in the Middle East and to speak on eschatological events and prophetic Scriptures: precisely the issues we had all agreed not to discuss. Surreptitiously, I looked around me. The response of the hearers was icy. Not a single voice was raised in assent.

"Lord, help us," I prayed silently, wishing I were anyplace else in the world but in that room.

But the worst was yet to come.

The man's final point sent shivers down my spine. "Whether we like it or not," he continued, "we must face and discuss the issue of the land of Israel, in the context and in the terms of Old Testament prophecy . . . and realize that when Jesus comes back, He will come back to this land!"

Unconsciously, I slid down in my seat, as though to shut out the devastating words I was hearing. But the speaker was not yet finished. Seemingly unaware of the destructive impact of his topic, he gave a detailed account of the most sensitive areas of Biblical prophecy and political ideology.

I knew that at that moment many of the delegates believed they'd been tricked, sold out. And that we'd brought them to this isolated island to expose them to the darts of the enemy. I felt like the cold hand of the devil himself was gripping my heart. "Dear Lord . . ." I prayed, "Dear Lord . . ."

After what seemed like an eternity, the minister stopped and sat down, smugly unaware or uncaring that he had lit a short fuse to a potential atomic bomb.

Not a person moved. They sat still, unmoving, as though they were paralyzed.

I didn't know what to do. In fact, there was nothing that I could do. Yet I knew that *something* must happen, because an explosion was sure to come.

John Wilson, who was moderating the meeting, came to the microphone and tried say something, anything that would pour healing oil on the troubled hearts of the delegation. But in that charged atmosphere, I could sense that his words were making very little impact.

Suddenly a Lebanese pastor leaped to his feet and literally ran to the microphone. Ignoring the feelings of the British clergyman, he shouted, "Please . . . don't move! Let's remain calm. Let us keep the spirit of the conference."

Then turning and addressing the speaker, he said, "We love you, Brother. Even though you don't realize how we see things."

Speaking again to the delegation, he pled, "Please . . . please, let's don't let our brother's unfortunate remarks destroy the congenial atmosphere we were beginning to build. Let's adjourn . . . drink a cup of tea . . . and pray for unity . . . please . . ."

With an apologetic nod in John Wilson's direction, the Lebanese pastor took his seat. John acknowledged the pastor's remarks, then with a smile and a shrug said, "I think that was what I was trying to say."

John's remark brought smiles and a smattering of laughter, and for the moment at least, the ice was broken. Nevertheless, as the room cleared, clusters of delegates gathered, some shaking their heads and muttering angrily.

With a heavy heart I arose and began pacing, pray-

ing quietly. At that moment I thought the entire conference had been ruined. Not knowing what else to
do, Heidi remained quietly in her seat.

Shortly two delegates approached us; one a Jorda-
nian, the other from Iran. "Keith, we've got to pray,"
one of them said. "Only God can help us now. It's
possible that this whole convention has just been destroyed!"

I nodded in agreement, and the four of us moved
to a vacant room and got on our knees. We prayed
earnestly and in one accord—binding the satanic
spirit that was attempting to gain foothold among us.
And we besought the Lord that he would bind the
conferees together in the same spirit of the unity that
Jesus had prayed for. After a long season of interces-
sion, we sensed that the Lord was in control of the
situation, and the peace of God swept over us.

Not until later did we realize fully just how close
we had been driven to the edge of the precipice. I
thought of that when an Arab brother said, "Keith, I
was amazed that the Arab delegates sat through that
session so quietly. I fully expected some of them to
shout the speaker down or walk out on him. And
since neither of those things happened, I know that
we are living in the very midst of a miracle."

I nodded in full agreement.

As soon as I could break away, I moved outside
and down to the beachfront for a much-needed stroll
in the clean, fresh air. Sometime later, greatly re-
freshed, I returned to the hotel where I was immediately accosted by a member of the Arab delegations.

He spoke abruptly, "The entire Syrian delegation is
leaving tomorrow morning . . ."

I was aghast. "Leaving? All of them? But, why?"

"They believe there's a spy in our midst . . ."

138

"A spy?" The information staggered me.

"Yes, a spy. And they're afraid that he'll report all of us to the Syrian government."

I realized the charge was serious. Since it is illegal for Syrians to be in the presence of Jews, I knew that if these men and women were reported they were in danger of facing prison sentences.

"Maybe it's a mistake," I said. "Perhaps it's only a rumor, a trick of the devil to divide the brethren. Please advise the brothers not to be too hasty in their decision to leave. Please, ask them to pray and consider the possible harm that could be done if they left."

He assured me that he would do what he could.

"Oh, Lord," I thought, when he had left, "is it possible that You have brought us together . . . only to allow us to be torn apart?"

Then my own good sense gave me the answer. Assuredly not! God was not the author of confusion. This was the work of Satan. Many of us had worked hard and long putting this conference together . . . and we had been faithful. Surely God would help us raise up a standard against the works of darkness.

And, indeed, our God *was* faithful.

Bishop Festo Kivengere from Uganda was the next speaker on the agenda. I hoped that God would use this man of God to tear down the high walls and fences that had been erected.

"We are not here as members of a defeated community," Bishop Festo began. "We are here as members of the One who triumphed over differences of all kinds . . ." He paused and warmed us with his smile. "Relax, Brethren . . ." he said, "Relax!"

I took a deep breath and tried to relax. I knew that if anybody could pull this group back together and begin rebuilding bridges, Bishop Festo Kivengere could.

The message the bishop delivered that day was from the Lord. As he spoke, it was as though God Himself stood in our midst and spoke words of love, of healing, of peace. And as Bishop Kivengere poured out his heart, it seemed that we could see the Lord. We felt the pain that our division would bring to Him.

And as we saw the Lord . . .

Fears began to dissipate.

The stormy winds of anger began to melt away, to be replaced by the balmy winds of the Holy Spirit.

And healing began to take place.

Now, finally, the stage was set for reconciliation. During the final day there was a great time of melting and weeping as God moved among us. Jews and Arabs embraced each other in tears, each telling what the Lord had done in their hearts.

"God has given me new eyes," one brother said brokenly.

"He has given me a new heart," said another.

I stood in awe as I witnessed the Holy Spirit at work.

One Jewish brother embraced me. "Keith, I can hardly believe what has happened to me this week . . ."

"Tell me about it," I said.

"I am an Israeli soldier," he said, "and I've flown many bombing missions over Syria . . ."

Momentarily overcome with emotion, he regained control of himself, then began again. "My heart was full of hatred against Syria because of what they'd done to Israel. But now that hate is all gone. God has dome something tremendous in my heart . . ."

He turned to go, then set his luggage down again. "Keith, when I return to Israel today, if I were to tell my friends that I had spent these days with Arabs and other Syrians, they would not be able to believe me." He smiled. "And if I told them that I had actually embraced a Syrian, they'd think I was mad."

We embraced again. "Shalom, Keith," he said.

"Shalom to you, my brother," I responded. And he was gone.

I found it difficult to believe that the conference was over. I stood at the hotel entrance, and bid farewell to most of the other delegates. As I watched them drive away to make their boat connection to Athens, my heart was full. The sparkling blue waters of the Mediterranean spoke of healing and peace.

A prayer of thanksgiving welled up within my heart. "Thank you, Lord . . . truly we've been in the midst of a miracle."

13

THE PROPHET'S WARNING . . . AND REWARD

The last piece of furniture was in place and the final piece of debris was picked up and in the wastebasket. I looked around me at the hotel conference room. Everything was finished. Despite myself, I sighed, then turned and stumbled wearily to my room. Without bothering to disrobe, I fell across the bed.

"I think I could sleep for a week," I said to Heidi, who lay motionless, her face to the wall. Her only response was a tiny nod. I pulled my feet upon the bed and closed my eyes.

I was thoroughly, totally exhausted.

Heidi and I had been on the road for almost an entire year, traveling from country to country doing the work of the ministry. And though we praised God for the victories won, the physical and emotional drain had been cumulative, and they had taken their

toll. But the pressures of the past few weeks—
especially the past few days—had somehow seemed
to be greater than all the other months combined.

It's almost over, I thought. Soon we can go home.
The immediate prospect of a couple of non-involved
days and the refreshment of rest and sleep would be
a gift from God.

But, try as I would, my mind was still in a whirl,
and I could not get to sleep. Finally, I arose quietly
so as not to disturb Heidi, and stepped out on the
balcony. Below me the usually serene Mediteranean
was white-capped and choppy. A brisk wind swelled
the sails of the intrepid boats that had ventured out
from the jetty. From where I stood, I could see and
hear the grey-green waves crashing on the beaches
and piers.

The sea is as restless as my spirit, I thought.

Nevertheless, the gusty breeze whipped across my
face and cooled me. And as I leaned over the railing,
I began feeling my tight shoulder muscles relax.

I quietly slid a chair close to the railing and sat
down, propping my feet against the rail. Unbidden,
the movie projector in my mind replayed the events
of the past months. As though through the eyes of a
spectator, I saw and heard segments of our diplomatic
encounters with church leaders in the Middle East. I
saw their eyes flash and their arms gesture as they
warned us of the "impossibilities" that lay ahead.

One by one, Arab and Jewish Christian leaders
paraded past me and I called them all by name.

Then the camera turned south to the great continent of Africa which Heidi and I had crossed and
recrossed. I beheld the schools, the churches, the college campuses, the bus stops, the factories and the

open air centers and the native huts where we had
witnessed and preached the undying love of God.

We had done our best to present the Gospel clearly,
forcefully, adequately. But had we really done our
best?

As I meditated, I heard God's voice to Ezekiel
booming across the Palestinian desert, and—across
the centuries—to me. "Son of man," God said, and I
knew He was speaking as much to me as to Ezekiel,
"I have made thee a watchman unto the house of Israel: *therefore hear the word at My mouth, and give
them warning from Me.*

"When I say unto the wicked, Thou shalt surely
die; and thou givest him not warning, nor speakest to
warn the wicked from his wicked way, to save his
life; the same wicked man shall die in his iniquity;
but his blood will I require at thine hand. Yet if thou
warn the wicked, and he turn not from his wicked-
ness, nor from his wicked way, he shall die in his iniquity; but thou hast delivered thy soul" (Ezekiel
3:17-19).

". . . if thou warn the wicked . . . thou hast delivered thy soul."

God's words. God's commands. God's will revealed
to His man. Plainly, unequivocally. Forcefully. "Go,
tell the people," He was saying. "Go, take My message to the nations."

Ezekiel had obeyed those commands of the Lord,
and had thus been vindicated. But what about me?

"Have I obeyed those commands?" I thought aloud.
"Have I properly shared the Good News? Have I
warned the wicked . . . and have I adequately demonstrated to them the way of forgiveness and the blessings of a life of wholeness . . .?"

Month by month, country by country, I evaluated the ministry events of this past year. "Did I do my best?" I asked the Lord.

"Did we see the results You desired?

"Could I have been more effective . . . more productive?

"Was I disobedient at times . . . fearful to step out in faith in particular areas?"

In his own day, I realized that Ezekiel must have asked the same questions of the Lord. What had been the Lord's response to him. And what was the Lord's response now to me? As though in answer, I felt myself blanketed by a serene stillness. I blinked back to the present and looked about me.

Where just minutes before the sea had been turbulent, it was now as calm as stormy Galilee became that day when Jesus commanded, "Peace . . . be still."

I turned and looked at Heidi. Her even breathing told me she had finally dropped into a deep, peaceful sleep. I was grateful.

A glint of sunlight caught a smooth swell and flashed across my face, momentarily blinding me and I was instantly transported to another locale. I heard the words of the Apostle Paul's defense before his Jewish brethren in Jerusalem . . .

"And it came to pass," he spoke, and they quieted down to hear his words, "that, as I made my journey . . . suddenly there shone from heaven a great light round about me. And I fell to the ground, and heard a voice saying unto me, 'Saul, Saul, why persecutest thou Me?'

"And I answered, 'Who art Thou, Lord?' And He said unto me, 'I am Jesus of Nazareth, whom thou persecutest.'

"And I said, 'What shall I do, Lord?' And the Lord

said unto me, 'Arise, and go into Damascus; and there it shall be told thee of all things which are appointed for thee to do.'

"And when I could not see for the glory of that light, being led by the hand of them that were with me, I came into Damascus. And one Ananias, a devout man according to the law, having a good report of all the Jews which dwelt there, came unto me, and stood, and said unto me, 'Brother Saul, receive thy sight.'

"And the same hour I looked up upon him. And he said, 'The God of our Fathers hath chosen thee, that thou shouldest know His will, and see that Just One, and shouldest hear the voice of His mouth. For thou shalt be His witness unto all men of what thou hast seen and heard. And now why tarriest thou? Arise, and be baptized, and wash away thy sins, calling on the name of the Lord' " (Acts 22:6-16).

Another flash of reflected sunlight leaped from a wave, catching me full in the face, momentarily blinding me, and I shielded my eyes with my cupped hands.

". . . a great light . . ." Paul had said. It had blinded him for a time and brought him to his senses, slowing him down long enough to hear what God was saying to Him. Was there a message in this for me?

I knew that God called each of His children and commanded them to "Go and tell," to become involved in His ministry of reconciliation. He had called Ezekiel. He had called Isaiah. The twelve disciples. And the Apostle Paul . . .

And this day on the balcony overlooking the now smooth and serene Mediterranean, I knew as never before that I was being confronted with the same challenge, the same charge to take that same message to all peoples just as they had.

# # #

"Sir . . . sir . . . here's your address," the driver said as the truck jerked to a sudden halt.

"What's that? What address?" I asked. Startled out of my reverie I shook my head and looked about me. Where was I?

"This is the office of Isaac Ababio. Isn't this where you asked to go? . . . Well, we're here."

The Mediterranean faded from my mind and I was back in Accra. Accra, Ghana. By now Heidi was back in the States. And I would be there within a couple of weeks.

I stirred myself. "Oh, yes. Isaac Ababio's office. I guess I've been daydreaming. Thank you, friend. Thank you." I was genuinely grateful. *He must have come to my rescue because my Father sent him,* I thought.

I leaned to pick up my luggage, then relaxed and straightened up. I had absolutely no knowledge of the locales where I would be preaching while in Ghana. But I had prepared my itinerary with care, praying over every step, every mile of the way. So, as God had always done, I knew He was guiding me here, even in this strange land.

After all, wasn't I a witness for Him? An ambassador? A watchman? And wasn't He guiding my steps as He had guided the steps of the "cloud of witnesses" that had gone before me?

Yes, I knew that He was.

I knew that was so: because there were hundreds of those living witnesses praying for me. Praying *and* believing that God would protect and guide me. Men and women, and young people who had stood beside me faithfully to make these trips and crusades possible. Even now some of those living witnesses were undoubtedly on their knees, interceding for me . . .

With that wondrous assurance, I was ready for anything my Father might send my way. A song of praise came to my lips. I hoisted my luggage and moved it to the office doorstep.

I raised my hand and rapped on the door. I was ready for *the world that is waiting*.

EPILOGUE

Keith and Heidi Hershey are continuing their ministry of sharing the redeeming love of Jesus and equipping indigenous Christian leaders for the work of the ministry. Ministry outreaches have already been conducted in nations of Africa, Europe, Central and North America, as well as the Mid and Far East.

Avenues of outreach now include international evangelistic crusades and teaching seminars, the International Sponsorship Fellowship (ISF), which underwrites the ministry efforts of indigenous village evangelists and pastors, and thus enabling them to fulfill God's call upon their lives. In addition, a new weekly television broadcast—"Celebration of Victory"—has been launched and presently being aired in African nations.

The Reverend Keith Hershey is founder-president of Mutual Faith Ministries, an international, interdenominational, non-profit missionary evangelistic organization.

For more information write:
Mutual Faith Ministries
P.O. Box 3788
Granada Hills, California 91344

Keith Hershey is a graduate of Azusa Pacific University and has done graduate study at Fuller Theological Seminary. Mutual Faith Ministries (MFM) was founded for the express purpose of helping unite believers worldwide into a mighty force, and assist them in "joining their faith . . . encompassing the world . . . bringing the message of redemption."
—Editors